D0786619

JOCHEN RINDT

By ALAN HENRY

PHOTOGRAPHS BY
DAVID PHIPPS

HAZLETON PUBLISHING

PUBLISHER
Richard Poulter

EXECUTIVE PUBLISHER
Elizabeth Le Breton

ART EDITOR
Steve Small

PRODUCTION MANAGER
George Greenfield

HOUSE EDITOR
Peter Lovering

PRODUCTION ASSISTANT
Deirdre Fenney

STATISTICS
John Taylor

The colour photographs appearing on the front and back covers
and pages 65–80 are by David Phipps, with the exception of page
65 (top), which is by the author.

All black and white photographs are by David Phipps apart from
page 18, which is by Alan Henry.

This first edition published in 1990 by
Hazleton Publishing, 3 Richmond Hill, Richmond,
Surrey TW10 6RE.

ISBN: 0-905138-79-1

Printed in England by BAS Printers Ltd, Over Wallop,
Hampshire.

Typesetting by First Impression Graphics Ltd, Richmond,
Surrey.

DISTRIBUTORS

UK & OTHER MARKETS
Osprey Publishing Limited, 59 Grosvenor Street
London W1X 9DA

USA & CANADA
Motorbooks International, PO Box 2
729 Prospect Avenue, Osceola
Wisconsin 54020, USA

AUSTRALIA
Technical Book & Magazine Co. Pty
289–299 Swanston Street
Melbourne, Victoria 3000

Universal Motor Publications
c/o Automoto Motoring Bookshop
152–154 Clarence Street
Sydney 2000, New South Wales

NEW ZEALAND
David Bateman Limited, 'Golden Heights'
32–34 View Road, Glenfield, Auckland 10

OTHER TITLES IN THIS SERIES

Nigel Mansell

Niki Lauda

Alain Prost

Gilles Villeneuve

Emerson Fittipaldi

PROLOGUE

There have been few more controversial personalities in World Championship Grand Prix history than Jochen Rindt. This tempestuous Austrian blended enormous zest for life, an irrepressible sense of humour, monumental arrogance and blinding self-confidence behind the wheel of a racing car into a heady cocktail of spectacular action. Among his contemporaries, he was regarded by many observers as the one who wouldn't survive the course. Yet when his death came, practising for the 1970 Italian Grand Prix at Monza which should have seen him crowned World Champion, it was almost certainly due to the mechanical failure he had been privately fearing for months.

He was 28 years old, at the absolute zenith of his career. Yet Jochen Rindt had possibly only scratched the surface of his potential as a Grand Prix driver. To heartbroken fans and supporters all over the world, he bequeathed a kaleidoscope of vividly contrasting memories.

This was the man who prompted Denis Jenkinson, the respected Continental correspondent of *Motor Sport* magazine, to bet his beard against him winning a Grand Prix. After Jochen won the 1969 United States GP at Watkins Glen in a Lotus 49B, 'Jenks' duly submitted his hirsute appendage to cold steel and the badger.

Jochen was the man whom Jackie Stewart respected and regarded above all other opposition, apart possibly from Jim Clark; the man reckoned by his Winkelmann Racing Formula Two team-mate Alan Rees to be on a par with Clark in terms of sheer speed. He was the man who drove Colin Chapman to the depths of frustration, yet whom the Lotus boss was passionately determined to hang on to at the end of the 1969 season. On a purely personal note, he was one of the key personalities responsible for firing the author's desire to somehow become involved in the sport.

For my Father

It was on 17 May 1964 that Jochen Rindt sprang to international prominence at Mallory Park in the 30-lap Grovewood Trophy for Formula Two cars. This Whit Sunday fixture was one of the prestige events on the British national calendar, the programme ironically opening with another victory for the man who would emerge as Rindt's great sparring partner as they matured to F1 stardom. After Jackie Stewart had duly won the Formula Three race at the wheel of his Tyrrell Cooper-BMC, the big boys came out to do battle. And the dynamic, unknown Rindt, with his black Brabham carrying minimal identification from Ford Austria, started from pole position.

Rindt lapped the tiny Leicestershire circuit in 52.4s, 0.2 second faster than Brian Hart's Cosworth-owned Lotus 22 development car, with Denny Hulme's Brabham and Jim Clark's Lotus 32 next up. All that effort went out of the window at the start when Jochen stalled his engine and his Brabham was almost rammed by Tony Maggs as the South African accelerated away in his Midland Racing Partnership Lola.

Hart charged off into the lead at the start, but Clark ran round the outside of him on the fast 180-degree Gerards right-hander on the third lap, and was not troubled again all the way to the chequered flag. Rindt recovered to third, behind Clark's team-mate Peter Arundell and ahead of Alan Rees in the Winkelmann Brabham.

Impressive though that performance may have been, Jochen hadn't yet got into his stride. The following day, at the delightful Crystal Palace circuit in south-west London, Rindt produced an even more sensational encore. The main event of this national meeting organised by the British Automobile Racing Club was the 40-lap Formula Two London Trophy, the preliminaries to which included two 20-lap heats.

As expected, Jim Clark's Lotus 32 sprang into the lead at the start of the first heat, but Graham Hill forced his John Coombs-entered Cooper-BRM ahead on lap three and stayed there to the finish. In the second heat Rindt gave a taste of what was to come in the final, dodging ahead of David Hobbs's Merlyn on the second lap to dominate the remainder of the race. Alan Rees sat glued to his tail throughout, waiting for the slip that never came. Rees, one of Britain's brightest young driving talents of the time, was highly impressed by what he saw.

Hill was on pole position for the final, but made a poor start and it was Rees who led away on the opening lap. Hill nipped into the lead on lap two, but Rindt followed him through to second place next time round. Graham's Cooper soon started to understeer dramatically, its rear anti-roll bar having come adrift on lap three, and Rindt began chiselling away at his precarious lead. To the amazement of the British motor racing establishment, this young Austrian with the crew-cut and the boxer's nose forced his way through into the lead on lap 15 and inched steadily away to win by 1.4 seconds.

Time and again the black Brabham seemed to totter on the verge of disaster as Rindt hurled it from lock to lock like a saloon car, but always he hauled it back from the brink. Clearly this man was something special. Watching from the spectator enclosure opposite the pits, a fortnight short of his 17th birthday, the author was understandably captivated by the atmosphere, the sense of occasion, the tremulous excitement. He could even forgive his father for reading his newspaper throughout...

Making his name. Jochen broadsides his Ford Austria-backed F2 Brabham ahead of Graham Hill in the John Coombs Cooper-BRM, en route to victory in the 1964 London Trophy race at Crystal Palace.

One man, however, already knew enough about Jochen Rindt to head the queue of his admirers. In the pits, hanging out his signals, was a wheeler-dealer-cum-F3 racer who had first seen Jochen racing in his native Austria and was absolutely convinced that he was the fastest thing going. His name was Frank Williams.

Twenty-six years later, I would sit in Frank's office at Williams Grand Prix Engineering and hear him enthuse about Jochen as if that race at Crystal Palace had taken place only the previous week.

'I was his number one fan,' Frank insisted, 'and proud to be so. To me, he was the fastest human being God has ever put on earth to drive a racing car. I saw him for the first time at Aspern, the airfield circuit near Vienna, the year before he came to Crystal Palace. He was hurtling round this flat-out corner in a '62 Cooper in a classic four-wheel drift on every effing lap.... I thought he was brilliant. And I went up to him and told him I thought he was brilliant afterwards. He liked that!'

It was symptomatic of the claustrophobic insularity which enveloped the contemporary British racing scene that few people at Mallory Park or Crystal Palace had heard of Jochen Rindt. But Frank Williams, as a member of that nomadic band of F3 privateers who traipsed round Europe trying to earn a crust, was much better versed in what was going on – and who was coming up.

Similarly, Frank's F3 racing pal Jonathan Williams (no relation) also recalls being impressed by Rindt during 1963: 'I first saw him in the Formula Junior race at Monaco that year. He did miracles with the ex-Bardi-Barry Cooper, which hadn't done anything up to that point ... he was right up there with Spence and Arundell.'

As an afterthought, Jonathan remarked: 'Rindt had a white E-type, pink shirts. I remember thinking, "Who the hell's that queer?"' Alan Bennett would have been proud of a line like that!

Jochen Rindt was born in Achum, northern Germany, on 18 April 1942 of a German father and Austrian mother. Both his parents were killed in an Allied bombing raid on Hamburg when he was only a year old, so he was subsequently brought up by his maternal grandparents in the sleepy provincial Austrian town of Graz. From the outset he was nicely placed from a financial standpoint, being due to inherit a share in an old-established Mainz-based firm of spice importers, Klein and Rindt. Indulged by his doting grandparents, Jochen grew into a wilful, difficult-to-control youngster who got up to some nerve-racking exploits on skis and sledges before finally becoming old enough to begin driving at the wheel of an elderly, inherited Volkswagen.

'I was always in trouble at school,' Rindt reflected two years before his death. 'This was partly because I didn't work very hard and partly because I was always fighting. On one occasion I almost ran down one of the teachers on my motor cycle, so in the end I got thrown out and went to England to learn English, but I spent most of my time sailing. I was staying not far from Goodwood and, one Saturday, I went to a club race meeting.... It looked marvellous!'

He and his close circle of friends – which included future BRM F1 driver Helmut Marko – had all become keen on motor racing and actually journeyed to the Nürburgring in 1961 to watch Wolfgang von Trips's Ferrari finish second to Stirling Moss's Lotus in the German Grand Prix. Short of money on this trip, they detoured to Mainz, where Rindt banged on the door of the family business, requesting a donation of funds. As his biographer Heinz Prüller recalls, the caretaker treated this tousle-haired youngster with more than a degree of understandable scepticism.

Having given Jochen the taste for motoring, the Volkswagen was duly pensioned off to be replaced by a Simca Montlhéry, the engine of which he had modified as heavily as his financial resources would permit. An old friend of his family's who had been a keen rallyist then fired his enthusiasm for motor sport. After Rindt had cut his teeth in the Simca, the Alfa Romeo dealer in Graz lent a hand, offering him a fully equipped Conrero-tuned Giulietta Ti at cost price, undertaking to service it free of charge providing the youngster did well in the first race of the '62 season at Aspern.

However unlikely it may have seemed at the time, Jochen duly assured himself of the Alfa dealer's support, winning the event outright and beating a handful of 3.8-litre Jaguar Mk 2 saloons in the process. In all, he drove the Giulietta to eight victories before moving into single-seaters at the wheel of a Formula Junior Cooper.

This was the machine Jochen acquired from Kurt Bardi-Barry, a Viennese rising star who was already dominating the limelight as Austria's most likely talent of the future. Fitted with a Superspeed-prepared Ford pushrod engine, the Cooper T67 brought Rindt his first international victory on 14 April 1963 at the Cesenatico road circuit in Italy.

The 21-year-old Austrian lad's performance was quite significant to those who bothered to look beyond the English Channel, for Rindt had beaten two of the most highly rated Italian contenders, Giacomo Russo (who raced under the pseudonym 'Geki') in his works de Sanctis and Corrado Manfredini, driving a Wainer. Bardi-Barry, meanwhile, having won the previous weekend's race at Vallelunga, near Rome, was finding his brand new Cooper Mk 3A something of a major handful at Cesenatico and disappeared into the straw bales.

Rindt would later finish third at Monza behind 'Geki' and Bardi-Barry, but his most promising moment came in the non-championship Austrian Grand Prix on the Zeltweg aerodrome circuit, where the Cooper was fitted with a pushrod 1500 cc Ford engine. Bardi-Barry had done a deal with F1 privateer Carel de Beaufort to drive one of the four-cylinder Porsche 718s fielded by the Dutch aristocrat's Écurie Maarsbergen. Yet Bardi-Barry's best time in the Porsche was not only 2.7 seconds slower than de Beaufort's best, it was 1.4 seconds slower than Rindt, who retired from the race with engine trouble.

Unhappily Bardi-Barry was killed in a road accident during February 1964, his car colliding with a tram in Vienna as he returned home after an evening at the opera, so Jochen Rindt was left to carry Austria's hopes into the international motor racing arena alone. For the '64 season Rindt, intent on graduating to the new 1-litre Formula Two class, spent a monumental £4000 of his inheritance on the Brabham-Cosworth SCA which would propel him into the limelight over that memorable Whitsun weekend. He was helped by Austria's FIA delegate, a Viennese clock-maker called Martin Pfunder, who pulled a few strings behind the scenes to move Jochen up the queue of hopefuls waiting for these machines.

Frank Williams, who was by then just starting what would turn out to be quite a successful business dealing in racing cars, arranged the delivery of Jochen's new Brabham, accompanying the Austrian's mechanic on the run to Vienna. With the racer hitched up behind a spanking new Ford Thames transporter, which had double rear wheels, the two men made an epic dash to Austria in little more than 24 hours, a record which Frank would subsequently hold up as an example of what could be done under pressure if ever any of his transporter drivers frowned at any proposed scheduling.

During the course of the drive Frank managed to snag the odd kerb with those double rear wheels, sustaining a couple of punctures. Nevertheless, he expected to be greeted with gratitude and appreciation by Rindt on their arrival.

Far from it, as Frank recalls with amusement: 'Of all the ungrateful bastards ... all he could say was, "Look, you've broken my bloody wheels. How much is that going to cost me?"'

Jochen received the car just in time to rush out to Aspern airfield for the Kurt Bardi-Barry Memorial event, lining up on the back row of the grid after failing to make it for practice. He retired from the race, but a fortnight later raised a few more eyebrows by finishing fourth in the Eifelrennen behind Jim Clark's Ron Harris Team Lotus 32, Richard Attwood's Midland Racing Partnership Lola (which had been the victor at Aspern) and Mike Spence in the second Ron Harris Lotus.

*At 22 years old, photographed in 1964, Rindt looks little
more than a schoolboy.*

Overleaf: *The spectacular style with which Jochen stunned
the motor racing establishment at Crystal Palace in 1964
was later moderated, but it is remembered with awe by those
who were there that day.*

Alan Rees has not forgotten Rindt's performance round Crystal Palace. 'I hadn't even met him prior to that race,' he says. 'He hadn't actually achieved much before, although I knew he had done pretty well at the Nürburgring, where he finished fourth.

'Nobody had taken him seriously prior to that weekend. I was very close behind him during the preliminary heat at Crystal Palace, and on every corner he did what looked to me like a half-spin. After pulling my foot off the throttle for about seven laps, I started to get the message that this bloke must have known partly what he was doing, and I thought, "Jeez, he's not going to lose it, even though he looks it every time," so I kept my boot in, even when he was sideways in front of me. From then on I tried everything to get past, but I just couldn't do it, so he won the heat.

'Jochen was supremely confident, the complete extrovert. He was obviously pretty serious about his racing, but his whole outward demeanour suggested he was only doing it for fun – and having one hell of a good time.'

Following this race the two men became quite friendly and, as the only two Brabham privateers who seemed to be achieving much, decided to collaborate informally. Thus at the super-fast Reims circuit a little later in the season Rindt and Rees towed round in each other's slipstream, guaranteeing that they earned good grid positions. Rees, as it transpired, won that race in a split-second finish from Jack Brabham's own works car, but Rindt got involved in the multiple pile-up which almost cost the life of works Lotus driver Peter Arundell and failed to finish.

At this time Rees was driving for a private team owned by Roy Winkelmann, a successful American businessman whose interests included the Armoured Car Company, one of the first high-security courier services to be established in England. In 1963 Alan

had been entered in this concern's name, but Winkelmann soon sold the business to Chubbs, the locksmiths, and it later passed into other hands to become Securicor. Winkelmann was also beginning to build up a commercial motor racing accessory business selling such specialist equipment as Bell crash helmets, for which it had the exclusive UK concession. 'Winks', as the team became known among the motor racing fraternity, would operate from workshops at Slough beneath the Windsor Lanes bowling alley, another of the boss's enterprises. It would play a crucial role in the future development of Jochen Rindt's professional career.

For the moment, however, Rindt continued his solo F2 career as an independent entrant/driver. He had retired with broken suspension at Avus after being beaten to pole position by Tony Hegbourne's Normand team Cooper-Cosworth, and, after his disappointing Reims outing, a third place behind Denny Hulme's Brabham and Jackie Stewart's Lotus at Clermont-Ferrand marked his only worthwhile result for the balance of the year.

It was at the '64 Reims meeting that Jackie Stewart first recalls meeting the man who was to become such a close personal friend in the years that followed. At the time he and his wife Helen were driving round Europe in their Mini, Jackie contesting various prestige F3 races with the Tyrrell Cooper-BMC squad.

'Jochen was more fundamentally polished and worldly than I was at the time,' he remembers. Over the next two or three years they would grow to motor racing maturity together, sharing the bond which so often springs up between contemporaries in any pursuit.

'In relative terms we were the hicks, the new boys,' Jackie says. 'Jim Clark, Graham Hill, John Surtees, Lorenzo Bandini … they were the big stars. We looked up to Jo Bonnier as the super international sophisticate. We were just a couple of youngsters sharing hotel rooms and meals, even going to a drive-in movie together on one occasion when the South African Grand Prix was held at East London. I mean, can you imagine that? We were really not very sophisticated at all!'

The summer of 1964 also saw Jochen make his Grand Prix debut, driving one of Rob Walker's Brabhams in the first World Championship Austrian Grand Prix, held on the tortuous Zeltweg airfield circuit. He used the ex-Bonnier BT11 powered by a BRM V8, qualifying a respectable 13th on 1m 12.0s compared with Graham Hill's BRM pole time of 1m 09.84s. On the grid he was ahead of such respectable runners as Bob Anderson, Giancarlo Baghetti, Trevor Taylor, Chris Amon, Mike Hailwood, Tony Maggs and Phil Hill.

Grand Prix debut. Concentrating hard at the wheel of Rob Walker's Brabham-BRM during the first World Championship Austrian Grand Prix on the Zeltweg military aerodrome, summer '64.

The Austrian new boy ran in midfield until, as Gregor Grant rather quaintly reported in *Autosport*, 'Rindt came into the pits, puzzled that his steering wheel seemed to have moved round several degrees ... Rob Walker's mechanics couldn't find anything wrong and put it down to a miracle!' Later, he prudently retired.

Rob Walker found him an absolute delight. 'He was all bounce and joy, a charming boy,' Rob recalls with obvious pleasure. 'He was really most attentive. After the race he kept ringing me up and asking whether he could drive for me in 1965, but I told him it would be best if he could get in at Coopers because they had a guaranteed entry as a works team.

'The other thing I remember – much later – is Jochen saying to me, "Rob, I want to be World Champion so much that I'm even prepared to drive for Lotus." And he did.'

Another consideration was that Jochen's burgeoning links with Winkelmann Racing meant that he was contracted to BP, while Walker's cars ran on Esso. As a consequence he languished in an uncompetitive Cooper, playing the number two role to Bruce McLaren, as the 1½-litre Formula One trickled towards its end. He may not have had the chance to show his potential on the Grand Prix scene, but his exploits with Winkelmann Racing left many people with no doubt as to his unbridled star quality.

It was Alan Rees who had suggested that, for 1965, Rindt should come in under the Winkelmann umbrella as half of a two-car team. On the face of it, this might have been interpreted as an unnecessarily benevolent gesture on Rees's part, pursuing as he was his own racing aspirations. But Alan never saw it that way.

'No, it never entered my head,' he grins. 'In my own mind I was going to be World Champion, so it didn't make any difference to me having Jochen Rindt in the team with me. I was going to blow him off anyway. The only reason I was in racing was to get to F1 and become World Champion. But, except on odd occasions, Jochen was quicker than me. We never needed team orders because he was always going to beat me anyway, as things turned out!'

Rees concedes that he won a few races, but regards that as barely relevant: 'What you've got to remember is that we had the best team, plenty of finance and we could have the pick of the cars available. It was always a Brabham (at least up to 1969), the money was self-generating and we had the best driver. It was really easy. I organised the team, so I knew what was required.'

Jochen's first season at Cooper proved extremely disheartening, for he was not short on confidence and quickly concluded that the machinery wasn't really up to the job. Certainly as far as the current formula was concerned, Cooper's great days had passed.

The team which had pioneered Grand Prix racing's central-engined revolution in the latter part of the previous decade was now struggling. John Cooper had been badly injured in a road accident during 1963 and was still recuperating when his father Charles died at the end of the following year.

In April '65 came the news that the Cooper Car Company had been sold to the Chipstead Group, a major car dealing concern partly owned by Mario Tozzi-Condivi, a charming and successful wheeler-dealer car salesman. Chipstead was in the company acquisition business and, with John Cooper slightly uncertain about which way to progress in the future, the famous F1 team had changed hands. This partnership was later joined by Jonathan Sieff, nephew of Marks and Spencer patriarch Lord Sieff, who had been a keen amateur racing driver in his own right until a very serious accident at Le Mans in 1961 at the wheel of a Lotus Elite heralded his retirement.

Through Tozzi-Condivi a deal was done with Adolfo and Omer Orsi, the father and son industrialists who owned Maserati, for the development of a 3-litre version of the V12 which had originally seen service in the Maserati 250F some seven years earlier. This would at least ensure Rindt had a pukka 3-litre F1 engine for his second and third seasons with Cooper, even though 1965 was effectively a wash-out.

In retrospect it was quite understandable that, while these elaborate plans for the new formula were being hatched, '65 was something of a transitional season. Team leader McLaren had his sights clearly focused on his own organisation's F1 effort in 1966, so Cooper muddled through the last year of 1½-litre F1 racing as best it could.

Jochen's first outing as a works Grand Prix driver came in the South African Grand Prix at East London on New Year's Day 1965. Driving a Cooper T73-Climax, he qualified tenth, some 3.2 seconds away from Jim Clark's pole-position Lotus 33, which proved a comfortable winner. Jochen lasted until lap 38, running in midfield, until the ignition failed. Jackie Stewart, also making his championship debut, finished sixth for BRM.

A distant seventh on aggregate followed in the non-title Brands Hatch Race of Champions, then disqualification for missing the chicane at Goodwood in the Sunday Mirror Trophy and a broken con rod in the Silverstone International Trophy. His first Monaco Grand Prix was even more of a disaster, Jochen failing to qualify after repeatedly complaining that his engine was badly down on power.

This seemed to some people at Cooper like an uncomfortable rerun of Phil Hill's complaints during the previous season. However, on closer examination chief mechanic Mike Barney discovered that Jochen's own mechanic had made some

personalised modifications to the Austrian's chassis, in order to facilitate fuel tank fitting. He had removed a lug supporting one end of the Bowden throttle cable outer sleeve, the idea being that he would fix the sleeve after rebuilding the car by taping it against the chassis tube which carried water for the cooling system. When the water heated up, the cable fixing slackened off, allowing Jochen's throttle only partly to open.

The unfortunate mechanic was immediately dismissed and team manager Roy Salvadori made it clear that Rindt's failure to qualify was simply not his fault. He also paid Jochen the start money he would have received had he qualified, a gesture which seemed to mollify the understandably indignant Austrian.

The only high spots of the season were at the Nürburgring, where Jochen survived to finish fourth, and at Watkins Glen, where he was sixth in the United States Grand Prix. If it had not been for his F2 performances, Jochen might have sunk without trace.

On a brighter note, Rindt's frustrating first summer of full-time F1 was punctuated by a dramatically successful first visit to the Le Mans 24-hour sports car epic. Although lukewarm about the race from the outset, Jochen agreed to drive a Ferrari 275LM fielded by Luigi Chinetti's North American Racing Team. He was paired with the genial, bespectacled Masten Gregory, a native of Kansas City who, by that stage of his career, had jumped out of more racing cars doing the wrong side of 100 mph than most people had enjoyed hot dinners. It seemed an extremely unlikely driver line-up with which to embark on this gruelling marathon.

Ranged against a duo of factory-supported 7-litre Ford Mk 2s driven by Bruce McLaren/Ken Miles and Phil Hill/Chris Amon, not to mention a horde of smaller 5.3- and 4.7-litre GT40s and the works Ferrari P2s handled by John Surtees/Lodovico Scarfiotti, Jean Guichet/Mike Parkes and Lorenzo Bandini/Giampiero Biscaldi, the NART entry looked like no more than cannon fodder. Add to that the fact that it was running on whatever rag-tail leftovers Goodyear could find for it, and the Rindt/Gregory challenge looked even more speculative. But Le Mans can unfold into an extremely strange event...

Goodyear's Leo Mehl described the race to *Autosport* magazine: 'The first day I was there this short Italian man came up to me. He said his name was Luigi Chinetti, that he was running a production Ferrari 275LM and that Mr Hartz [Vice-President of Goodyear's development team] had promised him that I would bring along some tyres for him. I told him that I didn't know anything about it. I said, "Well, we've got plenty of tyres for these big Fords, but we don't have anything that even fits on a 275LM..."'

Faced with Chinetti's persistence, Mehl decided to improvise. In case of rain, he had brought along a small batch of skinny rain tyres, so just to keep Mr Chinetti quiet he gave him a set of those to try. Amazingly, the drivers loved them...

During the opening stages the works Ford–Ferrari battle raged at the front of the field, but the NART Ferrari, having started from 11th place, had moved steadily through to eighth by the end of the first hour. Rindt did the opening stint behind the wheel, handing over to Gregory after about 75 minutes. Less than two hours later Masten returned to the pits to complain about a serious misfire. Jochen began to pack his bags, assuming this to be something serious like a broken valve.

In fact, it turned out to be an electrical hitch. The distributor was changed and the NART car lost half an hour in the process. By the time it was ready to return to the fray, Rindt had changed back into his everyday clothes and was in the paddock preparing to drive off in his hire car.

Leo Mehl: 'Fortunately Jochen's road car was blocked in. Masten had gotten in the race car and then somebody said, "Where's Jochen?" Well, Jochen had got the wreckers and they were moving cars in the car park, and one of the crew guys said, "Jochen, don't leave, man, you're up again soon."'

Gregory had resumed in 18th place and made a pact with Rindt that they would drive absolutely flat out for the remainder of the race. If the Ferrari broke, then so be it. By midnight on Saturday they were 14th and, with the Ford challenge now spent and the fastest works Ferrari P2s slowed by persistent cracking of their ventilated disc brakes, Rindt and Gregory found themselves moving up into second place by dawn on Sunday.

Ahead of the NART car was the similar private Ferrari 275LM entered by Équipe Nationale Belge for industrialist Gustave Gosselin and nightclub owner Pierre Dumay. With the works Ferraris out of contention, Maranello team manager Eugenio Dragoni sent word down to the NART pit that Gregory and Rindt should be reined in and not challenge the Belgian duo.

Four years earlier Chinetti had received a similar missive from the works Ferrari team when his NART Testa Rossa, driven by Ricardo and Pedro Rodriguez, came within an inch of thrashing the factory cars in the 24-hour classic. On that occasion the matter was resolved when the NART machine retired. This time Ferrari's US importer, a triple Le Mans winner himself in years gone by, just laughed at the suggestion.

Storming through the early-morning mist, Jochen and his co-driver thrashed the NART 275LM to within a few revs of its life. Running at Grand Prix intensity, it consumed six sets of tyres and brake pads during the course of this frantic chase. By mid-morning on Sunday its engine was down on power, its brakes and steering vibrating ominously. Yet Chinetti's two chargers were carving into the Belgian Ferrari's lead at four seconds a lap.

Finally, the Gosselin/Dumay 275LM threw a tyre tread, badly damaging its rear bodywork. By the time it was patched up, Rindt and Gregory were through into a lead they would not lose. Yet even in the last hour it seemed as though fate might conspire to thwart their efforts. The differential began to break up to the accompaniment of painful grinding and grating in the transmission. For the last few miles Gregory took to declutching and coasting through the corners, only gingerly applying the power when the car was pointing in a straight line. The differential broke up for good as Gregory drove it into the paddock after taking the chequered flag...

It was a happy day too for Leo Mehl, who breathed a sigh of relief that Goodyear had been able to accommodate the NART Ferrari with those wet-weather tyres. 'It was our first victory at Le Mans,' he beams, 'and I'll never forget it. I called Mr Hartz and said, "Mr Hartz, you remember Mr Chinetti?" He said, "Yeah, yeah..." I said, "You remember telling him that I would take care of tyres?" "Yeah, I do remember that..." I said, "I've got news for you; we won the race!"'

This success notwithstanding, Le Mans was definitely not Jochen's cup of tea. He never finished the race again. In '66 he shared a Ford GT40 with Innes Ireland, lasting only to the third hour before its engine failed, and the following year he was paired with Gerhard Mitter in a Porsche 907. Its engine broke a piston and Jochen didn't return to the Sarthe.

Rindt may have found Le Mans something of a trial, but the lure of dollars helped him overcome an inherent antipathy towards the Indianapolis 500. He first went there in 1967 to drive an Eagle, surviving an almighty wall-scraping inferno of an accident when its throttle jammed during qualifying. He was duly taken to hospital for a check-up, but in the cab of the ambulance, not on a stretcher. Legend has it he actually offered the ambulance driver a cigarette; he clearly needed it more than the unflappable Jochen! Although a replacement car was found, he was bumped from the grid.

Winkelmann Racing, meanwhile, was carving itself an enviable reputation as the team to beat on the Formula Two scene. Its Brabham-Cosworths were immaculately turned out by two highly respected mechanics, Australian Johnny Muller and Kiwi Peter Kerr, who is still working with Rees to this day. It was one of the best-financed operations of its kind. As Rees explains, money was the least of their problems.

'First of all there was BP Austria chipping in to have Jochen included,' he remembers,

'and then Firestone, plus the fact that we got plenty of start money and lots of prize money because Jochen was winning most of the races. It was all self-funding, really...'

The expanded, two-car F2 team had its first race outing in the Daily Express Trophy at Oulton Park on 3 April 1965 after the season-opener at Silverstone had been cancelled due to heavy rain. Rindt was eliminated by gearbox problems after setting fastest lap and his BT16 also failed to finish the British Autocar Championship round at Snetterton a week later, having started from pole position. Thus the team would sally forth to Europe before Jochen notched up his first victory for Winkelmann.

It came in July at Reims, where Rindt somehow managed to win despite spinning early on in the torrid temperatures, then Rees won at Enna-Pergusa in Sicily, conceding, 'I think Jochen let me have that one!' The two Winkelmann drivers found they had enough money left in the kitty for a short holiday in the fashionable resort of Taormina where Jochen discovered that Rees couldn't swim and, with malicious humour, spent most of the time trying to tip him out of their hired boat.

The first race of the 1966 F2 season was scheduled to take place at Oulton Park, where Johnny and Peter worked into the early hours installing a fresh gearbox in one of the new Brabham BT18s, Alan's Cortina GT providing the necessary illumination from its headlights. The Cortina never went as well again and, in any case, it was a wasted effort because the event was cancelled after race day dawned to reveal a covering of snow!

While Jochen was to enjoy better fortune in Grand Prix racing, the 1966 Formula Two season was largely bereft of results thanks to the arrival on the scene of the works Brabham-Hondas driven by Jack himself and Denny Hulme. There was little even the dynamic Rindt could do about such an obvious horsepower deficit, but he and Rees did manage to register an early-season 1-2 in the Eifelrennen on the Nürburgring's South Circuit on a weekend when the Brabham-Hondas were busy mopping up at Montjuich Park, Barcelona.

The Brabham-Honda steamroller was finally thwarted in unforgettable style in late October when the BARC ran its first Motor Show 200 meeting at Brands Hatch. This produced what Rees describes as 'one of Jochen's three very special displays'. From the start the battle was exclusively between Rindt and Brabham, Cosworth's Keith Duckworth having reputedly squeezed a few extra horsepower out of the Winkelmann SCA for this special occasion.

Rees: 'They were lapping Chris Lambert at about two-thirds distance, with Jack

Surtees's Ferrari 312 leads through Eau Rouge on the opening lap of the rain-soaked '66 Belgian Grand Prix at Spa (left), but the Dunlop rain tyres on Jochen's Cooper enabled him to surge through into the lead when the track was at its wettest (below left).

Rindt muscled the Cooper T81-Maserati into third place in the 1966 Monaco Grand Prix before an engine failure brought about his retirement.

aiming to go past on one side and Jochen almost alongside him. Lambert looked in his mirrors and saw only Jochen, so he moved over to the side Jack was coming through. Jack had to lift and Jochen squeezed through into the lead. Brabham remained right behind for the rest of the way, but there was no chance of his ever overtaking Jochen again...'

The advent of the Cooper T81-Maserati marked a definite upsurge in prospects for Jochen Rindt for, although another three and a half years would pass before he finally won his first Grand Prix, the Anglo-Italian hybrid was good enough for him to demonstrate his true potential as an F1 contender. Jochen's first outing in the T81 came at the '66 Silverstone International Trophy, on the memorable day when Jack Brabham's Brabham-Repco V8 blew away the much-fancied John Surtees's Ferrari 312 V12. Rindt finished a distant fifth, then ran as high as third at Monaco before his engine expired.

The opening lap of the Belgian Grand Prix at Spa-Francorchamps saw Jochen avoid the multi-car pile-up which eliminated nine cars in a sudden rain shower, only to gyrate madly through the Masta Kink at high speed when he lost control in the wake of Surtees's leading Ferrari. With the Cooper-Maserati on Dunlop full wets and the Ferrari on Firestone 'intermediates', John was happy to follow in Jochen's wheel tracks – literally – until the line dried sufficiently for him to push ahead unchallenged. Jochen, despite a troublesome differential, finished a super second.

Another outing in the wet: Jochen splashing to third place
in the '66 German Grand Prix with the Cooper-Maserati
(left), and sharing the rostrum (below left) with
first- and second-place finishers Jack Brabham and
John Surtees.

Jochen leads Jim Clark's Lotus 33-Climax during the
early stages of the '66 British Grand Prix at Brands
Hatch. At the end of the race he was behind the Scot
but earned two more championship points.

In close company at Monza with '66 Italian Grand Prix winner Lodovico Scarfiotti in the Ferrari. The race netted another fourth-place finish for Rindt.

Before the French Grand Prix took place at Reims three weeks later, Surtees had been through his much-publicised rift with Ferrari and, once the problem of clashing fuel contracts was sorted out, John joined Rindt and Chris Amon in the works Cooper line-up. Richie Ginther, on loan from Honda, had partnered Rindt at Monaco and Spa, but now the American had been called away by the Japanese company to continue development testing of its 3-litre V12.

Jochen finished fourth at Reims, fifth at Brands Hatch, then a strong third behind Brabham and Surtees at the Nürburgring. The fact that Surtees was now effectively asserting himself as the *de facto* team leader didn't seem to trouble Rindt in the slightest, the Austrian just happy that he was running somewhere near the front of the pack. 'Jochen was a nice lad,' recalls Surtees, 'and we got on well. He did his own thing and was pleasant to work with. No problem at all...'

Rindt then took a fourth at Monza before sitting behind Jim Clark's surprisingly durable Lotus 43-BRM H16 in the United States Grand Prix at Watkins Glen. All he had to do was to sit there steadily; the over-complex H16 always broke. Didn't it? Not on this rare occasion, so Jimmy won and an amazed Jochen followed him home as runner-up. It was scarcely believable.... Despite this disappointment, he finished third in the Drivers' Championship, beaten only by Brabham and Surtees.

One race that Rindt seemed certain to win was the '66 US Grand Prix at Watkins Glen (left), where he was holding a firm second place, confident that Clark's Lotus-BRM H16 would not last the course. It did – and Jochen had to be content with second!

Left: *Leading John Love's Cooper-Climax and Dan Gurney's Eagle in the opening stages of the '67 South African GP at Kyalami. Engine failure claimed the Austrian's Cooper-Maserati on a day when new team-mate Pedro Rodriguez survived to score a lucky victory.*

Rindt stands by the ungainly Cooper T86-Maserati prior to its debut in the '67 British Grand Prix at Silverstone. On the right of the picture is the team's junior mechanic Ron Dennis. Today he is Managing Director of McLaren International.

In 1967 the Cooper-Maseratis really began to lose their place in the pecking order with the advent of the Lotus 49-Cosworth and a more powerful generation of Ferrari V12s. Moreover, Jochen's irritation was compounded when, having had to watch as Surtees won in Mexico at the end of '66, his new number two, Pedro Rodriguez, plodded home to a lucky victory at Kyalami when the South African Grand Prix opened the '67 title battle.

Rindt's third season with Cooper saw his fortunes plunge dramatically, failing to be revived even by the introduction of the ugly, magnesium-skinned T86 which Jochen had at his disposal from the British Grand Prix onwards. Over 100 lb lighter than the T81 it displaced, it delivered him only fourth place at Monza. Rindt was so frustrated that his parting shot to Cooper was to help the Maserati V12 on its way when he realised it was on the verge of blowing up in the US Grand Prix. With consummate lack of tact, he confessed this misdeed to Heinz Prüller within Salvadori's hearing. It finished his three-year slog with Cooper on a suitably nervous note…

A fine study of Jochen at speed in the Cooper T81-Maserati. After Surtees moved to Honda at the start of 1967, the Austrian was the last really tenacious driver to represent the famous British team's fortunes prior to its demise at the end of 1968.

Of course, in F2 it was a totally different story. The start of '67 marked the arrival of the new 1.6-litre regulations and the advent of Cosworth's splendid FVA. Winkelmann armed itself with a couple of Brabham BT23s and duly went on the rampage.

Alan Rees: 'Jochen had really got there that year, and I think if he had had a proper F1 car he would have been World Champion. He had many close races with Jim Clark in F2 and invariably blew him off; I felt that Jochen had reached sufficient speed with a good car that he was genuinely a match for Jimmy.'

Altogether, he put nine stupendous race victories in the bag, winning the French and British Championships with ease. As *Motoring News* pointed out a few years later, had the World Championship points scoring system been applied to F2, Jochen would have scored 107. Nobody else would have scored more than 50.

The '67 season passed like a blur. The night after the British Grand Prix Rees recalls flying down to Tulln-Langenlebarn, the airfield circuit near Vienna, for another F2 epic less than 24 hours after the Silverstone race. 'Jack Brabham flew us down in his private plane,' Alan remembers, 'but before departing we went down to his house in Surrey and just sat for most of the evening. Jack could do without sleep and I've always reckoned that he was applying a little gamesmanship. Jochen wasn't affected – he won the race anyway – but I well remember it as the day I decided that I really didn't want to be a racing driver any longer...'

There was the overnight flight back from the Canadian Grand Prix at Mosport Park, enabling Jochen to weave that Winkelmann magic in front of the English crowds at the August Bank Holiday Monday F2 race at Brands Hatch. Always the dark-green Winkelmann Brabham with its blue-helmeted driver could be seen being thrown from lock to lock with a matchless dash of *élan* which entranced the onlookers. Surging on into '68 went the Winkelmann cavalcade, now with more backing from BP Austria, and a brace of the latest Brabham BT23Cs at its disposal.

Rees had spent the winter trying to regain his motivation, but it was becoming pretty clear that 1968 would be his final season. As was becoming the norm, Jochen won the Easter Monday Thruxton international, then scored a truly epic victory at Zolder after Brian Redman's Lola T100 had clipped his Brabham's rear wheel at the start of the second heat, Rindt pirouetting the length of the grid before shuddering to a halt. He ended up pointing in the wrong direction, but spin-turned the BT23C and chased after the pack. Victory in the first heat had already fallen his way, but an amazing charge through the field to finish third behind the Ferrari Dino 166s of Jacky Ickx and Chris Amon saw him emerge victorious on aggregate. His success was helped by the Belgian driver ignoring pit signals to allow Amon through into the lead, a move which would have guaranteed the New Zealander the win.

Winkelmann completed a final season in '69 with Lotus before it called a halt and Jochen began operating his own team as part of his new deal with Colin Chapman. Of Jochen's career tally of 29 Formula Two wins, some 23 were achieved at the wheel of cars fielded by Winkelmann Racing. They had been great times...

Jochen matured enormously during 1967 and '68, appearing more relaxed, and he became good-natured, easy-going and convivial company among those he chose to befriend. Long before joining Team Lotus he knew he had unlocked the secret of winning races.

'He had a great sense of humour,' recalls Rees, 'but he remained a tremendously hard

Jochen with his wife Nina and French journalist Jabby Crombac, a close friend.

person. The more you gave it back to him the more he liked it. Massive self-confidence, arrogant as hell ... but that really great sense of humour. You could laugh and joke with him all the time, no problem at all. You could say anything to him and he'd just laugh. He was totally confident; he never said it in so many words, but the whole tone of his personality reflected a belief that he wouldn't be beaten by anybody.

'We got on tremendously well. I don't think he and Nina really had a particularly turbulent relationship – no more than anybody else does – and I think there was an underlying sense of mutual respect. Nina was pretty tough, of course. She wasn't impressed with his money, either, because her father was very rich and she was an astute businesswoman. I think they were well suited, a bit volatile, perhaps, but not that much.'

Jochen's arrogance might have had an appealing timbre to his inner circle of friends and fans, but others found it less endearing. Denis Jenkinson was one. Long before he staked his beard against Jochen winning a Grand Prix in 1969, 'Jenks' had concluded that the Austrian had a rather abrasive personality which he personally found unattractive.

'I thought he was conceited and arrogant,' he reflected to the author in 1990. 'He wasn't like Keke Rosberg, for example, who was cocky and confident in a way that made you grin and say, "Look, there goes that cocky so-and-so." Rindt was bigheaded and I saw several examples of it.

'I was quite close to Porsche during the time Rindt was racing and I watched him testing one of the first F1 Cooper-Maseratis at Goodwood early in 1966 for the new 3-litre F1. Somebody asked him whether he was driving for Porsche at Le Mans and he replied sarcastically, "No, they don't want F1 drivers in their team." I thought, you arrogant so-and-so. I did not find him a likeable person.'

Ron Dennis, now Managing Director of the highly successful McLaren International team, was a junior mechanic on Rindt's Cooper-Maserati in 1967 and agrees with Jenkinson's assessment.

'Yes, he was arrogant and really didn't treat people properly,' Dennis asserts, 'especially the mechanics. I recall at the 1967 German Grand Prix Roy Salvadori telling him that he'd better hurry up and get ready because it was almost time for the start. Rindt just replied, "They won't dare start the German Grand Prix without me..." So one of the other mechanics looked up and muttered rather acidly, "Why don't you pop down the road with your helmet and fill it with ten pounds of potatoes?"

'I switched to Brabham in 1968, when Rindt moved across, but I didn't want to work with him. I went to work on Jack's car. No, I have to say I don't have great memories of Jochen.'

The spring of 1967 also saw him marry Nina, the daughter of Finnish millionaire amateur racing driver Curt Lincoln. A stunningly attractive blonde who modelled for all the glossy, upmarket fashion magazines such as *Vogue, Elle* and *Mademoiselle*, Jochen had first met her in Budapest in 1963 when she was 20.

A blustery, on-off courtship followed over the next few years, with an initial engagement between the two wilful youngsters failing after the immature Rindt tried to impress her with his money and celebrity status. They spent two years apart until Jochen met up with her again in New York at the start of 1966. Nina realised he had matured enormously and on 5 March 1967 they were married in Helsinki.

It was destined to be a stormy alliance right to the end of Jochen's life, as Jackie Stewart remembers: 'It was a turbulent relationship all the way to the end. Nina was a feisty, totally independent girl with independent means and had enjoyed a very successful modelling career in Paris, New York and Milan. Her father also looked after her very well. She knew what she wanted and where she wanted to go. Nina's never done what she's not wanted to. She's a tough cooky, no question.

'They used to have awful arguments, something I wouldn't ever have thought of having so publicly with Helen, for example. But it was a different mood. It was very chauvinistic in Scotland at that time. I mean, you got married and your wife didn't work. I thought Jochen and Nina were very Continental!'

Three years of sometimes promising, but generally disappointing performances with Cooper had been enough for Rindt. Inwardly, he felt he was ready to win Grands Prix, an awareness heightened by the fact that his young contemporary Jackie Stewart had first triumphed in such an event over two years earlier. While wrestling with the Cooper-Maserati throughout the first two years of the new 3-litre F1, he had sat and watched while Jack Brabham and Denny Hulme reeled off victory after victory in their lightweight, taut-handling Brabham-Repcos. So when Hulme decided to leave to join McLaren, Jochen was quick to accept Jack's offer to take over his cockpit.

Future prospects looked good despite the advent of the Cosworth DFV V8 the previous summer in the sensational new Lotus 49, for Repco had the more powerful four-cam type 860 engine up its sleeve. Sadly, in his wildest nightmares, Rindt could not have imagined how appallingly unreliable it would be.

As a racing season, what was to come would amount to an unmitigated disaster which effectively wiped out any prospect of Repco continuing as a Grand Prix engine manufacturer. Despite this, Rindt is recalled with tremendous affection by all the Brabham team members. That the Austrian was certainly happy in this environment can be judged from the enthusiasm with which he viewed the prospect of a return to the fold after a difficult first season driving for Colin Chapman in 1969.

Jack Brabham admits that he was attracted to Rindt because he admired the determination he'd displayed, both with the Cooper-Maseratis and the F2 Winkelmann Brabhams. Jack's designer and long-time partner Ron Tauranac shared this high opinion of the Austrian.

'Jochen was always very pro-Brabham,' he remembers with some satisfaction. 'When he was eventually offered a deal to go to Lotus for 1969, he came to us, told us what Chapman was offering, and said that he would stay with us for a fraction of that price. We really got on famously. We were watching our costs in those days and we used to share a room together for much of the year. He was a good bloke.'

For Rindt's part, he admired Jack Brabham enormously. Heinz Prüller explained: 'Jochen put his trust totally in Jack. He wanted to be like him because he admired his attitude towards motor racing, his dedicated professionalism. And of course, because Jack drove the same car as his other driver, Jochen found driving for Jack reassuring. It was a relaxed, pleasant relationship.'

Jochen used one of the regular '67-specification Brabham BT24s for the South African Grand Prix at Kyalami and opened his Brabham innings with a strong third place behind the Lotus 49s of Jim Clark and Graham Hill. Tauranac then completed the

A touch of opposite lock in the '68 Monaco Grand Prix, a race which saw Jochen's early retirement after glancing a wall.

Enjoying a light-hearted moment with fellow-drivers at the Kyalami Ranch, a stone's throw from the South African GP venue.

stressed-skin spaceframe BT26 (a halfway house on the way to the team's first
monocoque design two years later) to cater for the new Repco 860 which made its first
appearance at the Spanish Grand Prix, with Jack himself driving.

The fiasco surrounding the Repco 860's racing programme is best summed up by
John Judd, who worked for Brabham on this project: 'I'd spent much of the 1967 season in Australia developing the four-cam engine and, while the power output was OK,
when we came to racing it we found we'd a number of quality-control problems. Gudgeon pins, for example … we spent one weekend rushing round converting the
engines to take gudgeon pins from a Petter diesel. We also had a problem with the valve
seats. We went down to Járama for that second race at the start of '68 and Jack suffered
a failure, caused by a valve seat falling out – and Jochen started from the pit lane because
we were all having tea in the transporter, not knowing quite when the race was due to
start! Then we heard the cars going out on the warming-up lap.

'Eventually we sussed that Repco were making the valve seats out of the wrong
material and that they were shrinking. So on the night prior to the Belgian race we tore
down one of the 860s which had shown the first signs of trouble during practice at Spa.
Jack flew it home immediately after the session on Saturday. We didn't have the right
equipment, but we managed to remove the old valve seats with a radial drill, prepared
and fitted new ones and then cooked them in Betty Brabham's domestic oven…. She
woke about three o'clock in the morning and almost called the fire brigade because of
the fumes in the house…

'The engine was reassembled and then flown back to Spa sitting in the right-hand
passenger seat of Jack's Piper Twin Commanche…'

The whole season degenerated into a total disaster and the only time the four-cam
BT26s finished a race intact was in the washed-out German Grand Prix at a mist-
bound Nürburgring, Jochen and Jack splashing home third and fifth. But there was no
acrimony whatsoever within the team, no bleating or complaining from any member.
It was viewed as a communal problem which had to be solved for everybody's benefit.

Notwithstanding these difficulties, the BT26 was undeniably a quick car, Rindt
slamming round Rouen-les-Essarts and St Jovite to qualify on pole for both the French
and Canadian Grands Prix. But he finished neither race. A leaking fuel tank, caused by
a venting problem, scuppered his chances in France, while a combination of brake
trouble and overheating forced him out in Canada while chasing Chris Amon's leading
Ferrari.

'We had no aggravation with Jochen at all,' says John Judd warmly. 'He was a bloody

*On pole for the '68 Canadian GP at St Jovite, Jochen's
Brabham BT26 (left) is beaten off the line by Chris Amon's
Ferrari and Jo Siffert's Rob Walker Lotus 49B. Again the
race ended in retirement for the bi-planed Brabham
(below left), this time with brake trouble and overheating.*

*Jochen with Brabham designer Ron Tauranac (left) and
Australian enthusiast David McKay (centre), himself a
keen Brabham privateer.*

good sport. Sure, he got browned off with everything, but he knew we were working very hard on that engine. As an indication of the atmosphere in the team that year, after all the problems we experienced during the Dutch Grand Prix at Zandvoort, Jack, Jochen, Ron and myself took over the dodgems down in the town for half an hour to get away from it all. It was a great laugh. Can you imagine Bernie Ecclestone or Ron Dennis on the dodgems? Neither can I...'

In 1968 Jackie Stewart moved his family from Scotland to Switzerland and the Scot would also find a house for the Rindts who, up to that point, had been enjoying married life in Paris. 'To start with I found them a small house very close, about 400 metres from the entrance of our drive,' Jackie recalls. 'It was nice, but not the way they wanted it. From there they moved into "Le Muids", a villa owned by Ingemar Johansson, the former World Champion boxer. At the time of Jochen's death in 1970 they were in the process of building a new property on a piece of land bought from Jo Bonnier...'

On 7 August 1968 Jochen and Nina became proud parents with the birth of their daughter Natascha Jonin. She would be their only child.

Before Rindt made the move to Team Lotus, his close friend and mentor Alan Rees retired from the cockpit after shuffling half-heartedly through the 1968 Formula Two season. His final few races were during the Argentine Temporada series late that year, when F2's regular front-runners found themselves commandingly outclassed by the suspiciously dominant Ferrari Dino 166s driven by the likes of talented journeymen Andrea de Adamich and Tino Brambilla.

At San Juan, in the Andes foothills, Jochen and Nina decided to make an excursion into the mountains and the Austrian missed first practice. 'Jochen figured he only needed the one day to learn the track and put in a decent time,' Rees recalls. 'But the trouble was a terrific wind blew up overnight, scattering sand and dust all over the circuit. Jochen went out on the second day, but it might as well have been on a wet track.' As a result, for the only time in their years together, both Winkelmann drivers started side by side on the back row of the grid.

'The flag dropped and Jochen was gone. He passed four cars before we got to the first corner. That was the last I saw of him until he came past me again about thirty laps later. By then he was third. But there was nothing he could do about those Ferraris. Boy, were they something else!'

Turning to the 1969 season, it is worth recalling the situation at Lotus when Rindt signed for the team. Remember, less than a year had passed since the tragic death of

Here we go again. Rindt wins the first F2 international
to be held at the newly reopened Thruxton circuit, at
the wheel of the Winkelmann Brabham BT23C, on
Easter Monday 1968.

Jim Clark – the man with whom Chapman had risen to Grand Prix fame and by whose standards all other F1 drivers of his era were judged – at Hockenheim on 7 April 1968.

Chapman, of course, had regarded Clark as a close friend. They talked the same language, enjoying an almost telepathic degree of communication on technical matters. And Jimmy was the ultimate car conserver: smooth, delicate of touch, an overwhelmingly natural driver. After his death Graham Hill had carried aloft the fallen Lotus standard to win the 1968 championship titles, but close scrutiny of the results reveals how lucky he was that Jackie Stewart had a troubled maiden year with the Tyrrell Matra.

The Lotus founder had made overtures to Stewart since 1964, but the 'other Scot' had resolutely declined to join the Lotus enclave. In the wake of Clark's death, Mario Andretti had driven one of the Lotus 49Bs in the 1968 United States Grand Prix at Watkins Glen and rocked the F1 fraternity by starting from pole position.

In addition to signing Rindt alongside Hill for '69, Chapman invited Mario to do as many Grands Prix in a third entry as his USAC schedule would permit. Jochen was not terribly impressed by this decision to stretch the team's resources, but he was keen to be behind the wheel of a competitive Cosworth DFV-engined car at last, so he just got on with it.

Further complicating Jochen's relationship with Chapman was the Lotus chief's burning commitment towards the development of the four-wheel-drive type 63. The '69 season would see his team, Matra, McLaren and Cosworth all experimenting with such design concepts, yet the advent of high-downforce aerofoils would render them obsolete and impractical almost from the outset. Rindt's reluctance to co-operate with Chapman on this project was another major source of friction between the two men.

Before tackling any F1 commitments for his new team, Rindt joined Graham Hill for the Tasman series in Australia and New Zealand. They were equipped with a brace of what were originally '67-spec Lotus 49s powered by Cosworth V8s, the short-stroke crankshafts of which reduced their capacity to 2.5 litres. One of these was replaced by a 49B in time for Jochen to drive it in the third race after he had rolled his original machine, writing it off, during the event at Levin in New Zealand. He then recovered form to win the Lady Wigram Trophy at Christchurch and the Tasman International 100 at Sydney's Warwick Farm circuit.

Chris Amon, who won the Tasman title in a Ferrari Dino 246, recalls Jochen with great affection, but confesses that he hated the way in which the Austrian, along with his pal Piers Courage, behaved like a pair of elitist bores throughout the winter series. They never carried on like that in Europe, he remembers.

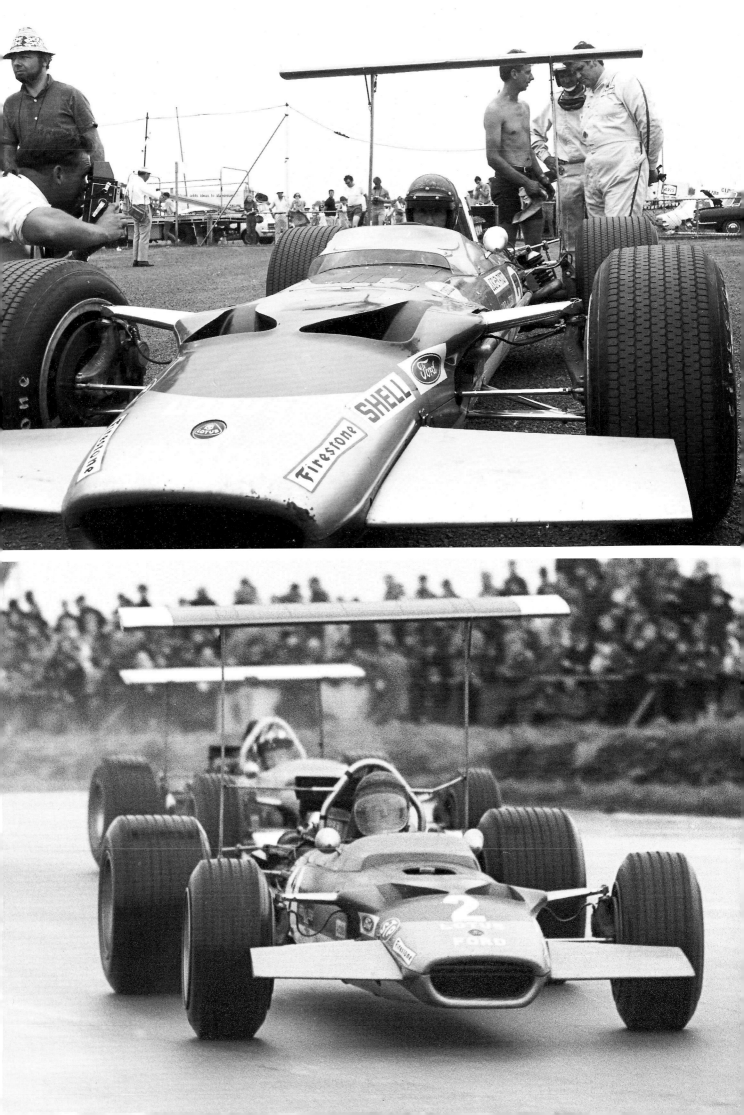

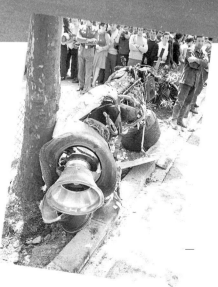

Top: *Colin Chapman superintends the fitting of a tailpiece to the high wing on Jochen's Lotus 49B prior to the near-tragic '69 Spanish GP at Barcelona. Mechanic Dave Sims tries to hide his doubts…*

In the opening stages of that race, Jochen surged away from Chris Amon's Ferrari and the rest of the pack, but his day ended in disaster when the wing collapsed and he crashed heavily.
Right: *The mangled Lotus monocoque lies by the side of the circuit.*

60

Jochen's first outing in the F1 Lotus 49B came at Kyalami for the South African Grand Prix on 1 March. He qualified second to Jack Brabham's Brabham BT26A-Cosworth, and comfortably ahead of both Hill and Andretti. He briefly held second place in the early stages before dropping back into the middle of the pack, eventually retiring with mechanical fuel pump problems.

Before the start of the European season Jochen scored a memorable second place in the Silverstone International Trophy race, almost catching Brabham's out-of-fuel BT26A in a last-lap sprint. The race took place in torrential rain and the Austrian stooged round near the back of the field until his 49B's Cosworth V8 eventually cleared a misfire and began to run on its full quota of cylinders. From then on, it was pure Rindt dynamite...

Spectating at Stowe was an enthusiastic Nigel Roebuck, today Grand Prix Editor of *Autosport*. 'On one lap I remember Brabham coming down into Stowe followed by Courage and Ickx, who were dicing for second place,' he recalls. 'They were just about to lap Hill and Pedro Rodriguez's BRM, and Jochen was behind them all. He disappeared into Stowe in a cloud of spume in fourth place, and came out second. In what seemed like a split second, he'd not only overtaken two cars, but managed to lap two more. Don't ask me how he did it...'

The European season kicked off at Barcelona's spectacular Montjuich Park circuit, where Jochen blitzed the opposition to take pole by half a second. But this event marked a precarious high point in F1 technical development where one's competitive standing in the paddock was measured in terms of the size of one's rear aerofoil. Predictably, the Lotus 49Bs appeared with the tallest, most spindly concoctions in the business.

At the start Rindt tore away from Amon's Ferrari, Jo Siffert's Rob Walker Lotus and the second works 49B of Graham Hill. Hill quickly moved up into third place, but as early as lap nine his rear aerofoil collapsed as he crested the rise just beyond the pits and he was pitched into the guard rail, tearing both front wheels off in the ensuing impact.

Graham instantly realised that the wing had collapsed and the sight of Jochen's progressively buckling under load as he came over that brow time after time alerted the veteran English driver to the possible danger. Too late, he despatched one of the team's mechanics back to the pits to have Rindt called in...

Going into lap 20, the same fate befell Jochen's machine, but he spun even more luridly and cannoned off the wreckage of Hill's car, coming to rest upside down in the middle of the road. Hill was first to arrive on the scene, turned off all the switches and helped to extricate Jochen, who was bleeding profusely from a broken nose, from the remains.

Suffering from serious concussion, he was admitted to a Barcelona clinic under the care of Spanish racer Alex Soler-Roig's father, a distinguished surgeon, and had to miss the forthcoming Monaco Grand Prix. Richard Attwood took his place, finishing fourth while Hill won what would turn out to be the final F1 championship victory of his career. Thankfully, Monaco also saw the sport's governing body – the CSI – intervene to outlaw those high aerofoils overnight.

During his stay in hospital Rindt wrote an open letter to all European motoring journals urging that wings should be banned on safety grounds, a move which irked Chapman considerably. He also expressed his gratitude to the organising club for having recently installed guard rails at that point on the circuit. Without them, he rightly reasoned, he would have been killed; of that there was no question in his mind. As a tangible gesture of appreciation he commissioned Viennese jeweller Gotfrid Köchert, whose Ferrari 275LM he had once driven to an outstanding sports car victory on the Zeltweg airfield, to make a silver facsimile of a piece of double-height guard rail which, appropriately inscribed, was presented to the Automobile Club of Cataluña.

Motor Sport magazine, almost predictably, was the sole journal which declined to publish Rindt's letter, thereby depriving itself of a slice of Grand Prix history. Moreover, it was at Monaco in 1969 that Denis Jenkinson finally tired of hearing from other people just how wonderful Jochen Rindt was. 'I was sitting at a street café having a meal,' he recalls, 'when I struck up a conversation with Robin Richards, the commentator, and John Webb of Brands Hatch on the subject of Rindt. To be honest, I was a little bored with the way it had suddenly become fashionable to be a Rindt fan and we got into a bit of an argument about it.

'Finally I said I'd bet my beard he wouldn't win a Grand Prix in 1969. So we wrote the deal on a paper tablecloth, all duly signed and sealed, and, on the day after Rindt won at Watkins Glen, I shaved it off, put half in an envelope which I sent to John Webb, the other half in an envelope to Robin Richards. Webb's half was embalmed in plastic and mounted on the Brands Hatch clubhouse wall, while the other half was mounted and auctioned at the Doghouse Club ball the following winter...'

Jackie Stewart: 'The Lotus 49B suddenly enabled him to come of age as a driver. I don't think there was much question that it was the best car, and he lost that extrovert exuberance that had characterised his style in F2. My Tyrrell Matra may have been the best-built, nicest-engineered machine, but the Lotus had the ultimate edge. And he was no slouch.

'With that in mind I just couldn't understand why Jenks wrote that. To me, it was so obvious that Jochen was going to be an extremely significant racing driver. Jenks had said some radical things before on the safety matter, so I personally was wary of his judgement, but I didn't think this was at all astute of him. None of the other drivers doubted Rindt had the ability. In 1969 and '70 he had matured into as good a racing driver as I ever raced against during my career.'

Understandably, Rindt had his enthusiasm for Denis Jenkinson pretty well under control. 'Once he made up his mind that he wasn't going to get on with somebody he would cut them out completely,' Jackie remembers. 'He would carry on a conversation with a third party while standing alongside the offending individual, treating him as if he just didn't exist. In some ways I admired him for that unwavering single-mindedness.'

On 5 May 1969 Jochen wrote to Colin Chapman at the Howard Johnson Motor Lodge at Indianapolis highlighting his concern about what he saw as the unacceptable fragility of the current breed of Lotus racing cars. This letter was regarded as so controversial and sensitive at the time that Chapman's lawyers insisted on its removal from the English translation of Heinz Prüller's official Rindt biography in 1971.

'Now to the whole situation, Colin,' wrote Jochen. 'I have been racing F1 for five years and I have made one mistake (I rammed Chris Amon at Clermont-Ferrand) and I had one accident at Zandvoort due to gear selection failure. Otherwise I stayed out of trouble. This situation changed rapidly since I joined your team – Levin, the Eifelrennen and now Barcelona.

'Honestly, your cars are so quick that we would still be competitive with a few extra pounds used to make the weakest parts stronger ... please give my suggestions some thought. I can only drive a car in which I have some confidence and I feel the point of no confidence is quite near.'

*The making of a name. Jochen receives the London
Trophy at Crystal Palace, Whit Monday, 1964, after
exploding into prominence with an unexpected victory.*

*First year in F1. Jochen looks slightly preoccupied at the wheel of the 1½-litre
Cooper-Climax during the 1965 British Grand Prix at Silverstone, a race which
produced just another retirement in a season-long catalogue of disappointment.*

Left: *Rindt struggles with the unwieldy Cooper T81-Maserati during the 1966 French Grand Prix at Reims, a race won by future team-mate Jack Brabham's Brabham-Repco.*

Close-up of Rindt at work in the Cooper-Maserati at Brands Hatch during the 1966 British Grand Prix. He finished fifth.

Left: *Unlikely second place. Jochen was amazed not to inherit victory in the '66 United States Grand Prix, but Jim Clark's mechanically complex Lotus 43-BRM H16 kept running, against the odds, in front of the Austrian.*

Looking sceptical. Rindt chatting with 1967 Cooper team-mate Pedro Rodriguez (left) and team manager Roy Salvadori.

Right: *A touch of opposite lock with the now-ageing Cooper T81 during the 1967 South African Grand Prix. Jochen later retired and Rodriguez scored a lucky win.*

Rindt's sole finish in the points with the four-cam Repco
860 engine came in the rain and mist at the Nürburgring
(opposite), where his Brabham BT26 splashed home
third in a race won by Jackie Stewart's Matra.

Jochen with Jack Brabham. The Austrian felt
extremely comfortable in Jack's team, and gave serious
consideration to rejoining the constructor/driver
for 1970.

Left: Rindt's last outing in an F1 Brabham came in the
1968 Mexican Grand Prix. As usual, the BT26 failed
to last the course, with ignition trouble sidelining it on
this occasion.

The day that Jenks's beard was doomed! Jochen heading
for victory in the 1969 United States Grand Prix with
the works Gold Leaf Team Lotus 49B.

*Colin Chapman despaired of Rindt on some occasions,
unable to reproduce the harmonious, easy-going
partnership he had enjoyed with the late Jim Clark.
Stern-faced paddock confrontations like this between
Jochen and the Lotus chief were commonplace.*

Last anniversary. Rindt's final F2 appearance at Crystal Palace, six years after his historic first win, at the wheel of his works-backed Jochen Rindt Racing Lotus 69.

However much Rindt may have annoyed his critics, his face inevitably wore the relaxed expression of a man at peace with himself, and content with his own way of doing things.

Left: *Rindt in extremis with the Lotus 49C, wound up in pursuit of Jack Brabham in the closing stages of a gripping 1970 Monaco Grand Prix.*

Lucky win. Rindt's triumph in the 1970 French Grand Prix at Clermont-Ferrand was made easier when trouble hit Chris Amon's March and the Matra of Jean-Pierre Beltoise.

Left: *Overshadowed victory. Jochen en route to his first win with the Lotus 72 in the Dutch Grand Prix at Zandvoort, an achievement rendered joyless due to the death of his close friend Piers Courage in the same event.*

Overleaf: *As British fans will remember him. Jochen heading for victory in the 1970 British Grand Prix at Brands Hatch – but only after Jack Brabham ran short of fuel in the closing stages.*

*Delayed concussion caused by his earlier accident at
Barcelona left Rindt suffering from acute nausea in the '69
French Grand Prix which the ups and downs of the
Clermont-Ferrand circuit served to aggravate. In an effort
to get more fresh air, he abandoned his recently adopted Bell
Star helmet for this open-faced version borrowed from his
friend Piers Courage.*

It was simplistic stuff by the standards of F1 engineering today, but scotched the fashionable view that Rindt was totally without fear. 'A lot of people think I'm braver than Dick Tracy,' he mused, 'but I can be just as scared as anybody...'

Jochen was back in the cockpit for the Dutch Grand Prix at Zandvoort, where he wore an all-enveloping Bell Star helmet for the first time, with a sticker reading 'This $pace [sic] to let' on either side. Again, he hurtled away into the distance only for a driveshaft coupling to shear. Stewart won his third victory of the year.

In the French Grand Prix Jochen found the switchback of Clermont-Ferrand absolutely impossible to manage, suffering as he was from delayed concussion in the aftermath of the Barcelona shunt. Abandoning his Bell Star, he borrowed a spare open-faced helmet from Piers Courage, but lasted only until lap 23 of the 38-lap race before double vision and sickness compelled him to retire. He apologised profusely to Chapman, who accepted with good grace. It was Colin's damned aerofoil experiments which had got Rindt into this state anyway...

*Jochen's last Grand Prix victory, barely a month before his
death, came in the German GP at Hockenheim. Here he
leads the Ferrari 312B1 of his great rival Jacky Ickx,
whom he outmanoeuvred on the last lap to score a
memorable victory.*

Finally, in the British Grand Prix at Silverstone, Jochen began to show his genuine world-class potential, even though the weekend got off to a shambolic start. Lotus didn't even bother to turn up for first practice, and when it did it clearly expected Rindt and Hill to handle the 4WD type 63s, having negotiated the sale of its 49Bs – only two of which remained in stock after the Barcelona write-offs.

Rindt said he wasn't driving a 63 under any circumstances, and one of the 49Bs had to be borrowed back from its 'new' owner Jo Bonnier, the Swede meekly accepting a loan of one of the 63s for the Silverstone event. Frankly, the whole weekend was chaotic for Lotus. 'Like Barnum and Bailey in two separate rings,' snorted Jochen unsympathetically.

Highly motivated, Rindt took pole position by 0.4s from Jackie Stewart's Matra MS80 and, from the outset, the 84-lap race erupted into a battle between these two superstars. Jochen led the first five laps, then Stewart slipped past for ten laps before Rindt began to assert himself firmly at the head of the field. Right through to lap 62 the dark-blue-helmeted driver kept the Lotus 49B in front ... until a rear wing end plate worked loose and began to foul a rear tyre.

Stewart pulled level with him and signalled that he was in trouble. Jochen hurtled into the pits where the offending end plate was torn off and he resumed second, now almost half a minute behind. Denis Jenkinson has mused: 'Moss, Clark, Andretti or Villeneuve wouldn't have stopped in those circumstances.'

Finally, just to cap a shatteringly disappointing weekend, Jochen ran low on fuel and had to stop again for a top-up. He finished fourth. Now it was Chapman's turn to apologise. But Jochen had proved himself.

'He got away from me at one point,' says Jackie Stewart, 'and initially I couldn't catch him. Then I did catch him and could see that he was driving technically very well indeed. There was no sideways stuff that day. When his rear wing end plate came loose and began dangling, I was genuinely worried that it would puncture his rear tyre. I'm not sure he could see it in his rear-view mirror. That was a race in which I think either of us would have been quite happy to finish the day with second place. In the end, of course, it didn't affect the outcome, because he ran out of fuel...'

Silverstone was probably the lowest point in the Chapman/Rindt relationship, but things began to get better from that point onwards. Jochen would eventually be cajoled into driving the unloved 4WD Lotus 63 in the non-title Oulton Park Gold Cup meeting, where he finished second to Stewart's Matra. But he never raced the car in championship action; that privilege was reserved for the team's occasional third driver John Miles.

Right: *The battle for the lead at Monza, '69. Stewart just leads Rindt, Courage, Jo Siffert's Lotus 49B and the rest of the pack.*

Below right: *Tension in the pits. Graham Hill and Jochen Rindt talk earnestly with Colin Chapman while the team's third driver John Miles* (right) *tries to keep out of it.*

Ahead again for Lotus. Jochen's 49B takes an immediate lead at the start of the '69 Italian GP at Monza, with Stewart's Matra (no. 20), Piers Courage's Frank Williams Brabham (no. 32) and Bruce McLaren's McLaren (no. 18) leading the pursuit. Jochen was beaten into second place by the Scot by less than a length.

In the Italian Grand Prix at Monza, Jochen was beaten into second place by Stewart's Matra by eight-hundredths of a second, Jackie having prepared his whole weekend with that final sprint to the line in mind. It clinched the Scot's first World Championship. He ran a particularly long fourth gear which he knew would save him one change in that last-lap drag race. Jackie recalls Jochen being 'rather angry' after he had taken the chequered flag 'because I don't think his pit signals had made it clear to him that this was the final lap'.

Jenks's beard was beginning to look safe after all but, following a third place in Canada, Jochen finally made it to the winner's circle with a masterly drive at Watkins Glen. Stirling Moss wrote to him: 'I have seen many great Grands Prix, but I reckon yours equals any of them.' He had got the better of Stewart's Matra early in the race and, after Jackie retired, stroked home to an easy victory ahead of Piers Courage in the Frank Williams Brabham. Snip, snip, snip...

Although Jochen had finally won his first Grand Prix during his maiden season with Team Lotus (in a race which sadly saw team-mate Graham Hill sustain serious leg injuries), he still remained apprehensive and unconvinced about Colin Chapman on a personal basis. The two men had professional respect for each other, but only bumped along on a personal basis. The near-tragedy at Barcelona and the farce at Silverstone surfaced in Rindt's mind time and again. He felt Team Lotus was a bit of a shambles. But Chapman now knew that Jochen was extremely quick. He might lack the finesse of Jim Clark, but those lightning reflexes produced spectacular results.

Celebrating the great moment with his friend Piers Courage, who finished second at the wheel of the Frank Williams Brabham.

Nevertheless, there were strong overtures from Jack Brabham. His team had now switched to reliable Cosworth DFV power and might provide just what Jochen was looking for: an uncomplicated, vice-free, durable chassis with a solid, reliable engine. Moreover, had Rindt rejoined the team, Brabham would have retired from driving.

Bernie Ecclestone, who by now was managing Jochen's business affairs and was Natascha's godfather, found himself stuck right in the middle of this dilemma. Bernie realised that the Austrian could be quite a sentimental soul in some ways and fully appreciated just how important it was to him to be comfortable in his relationship with the team for which he drove. But he also understood that Chapman was prepared to bid the earth to keep Rindt in his team.

Bernie got in touch with Goodyear in an attempt to put together a realistic package which would enable Jochen to return to the Brabham fold, but Chapman trumped the whole proposed deal with more money and the promise of his own F2 programme, using the new Lotus 69. Winkelmann Racing, which had switched from Brabham BT23Cs to Lotus 59s when Jochen moved to Chapman's squad at the start of '69,

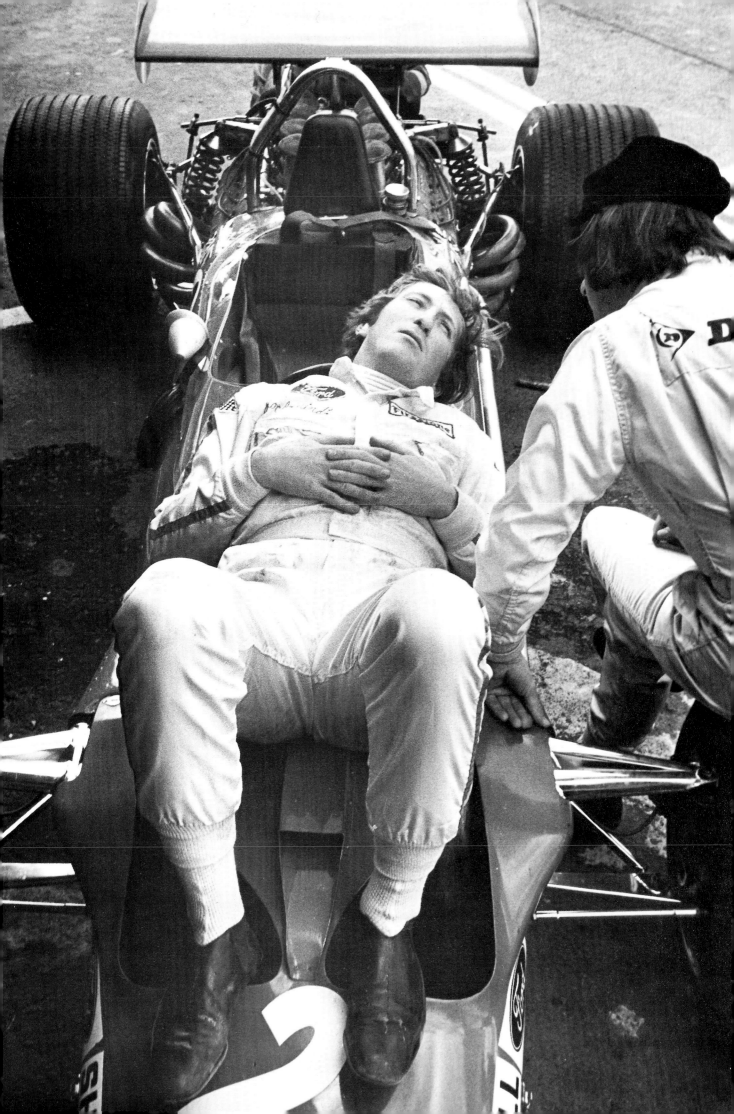

ceased operating at the end of that season when Alan Rees became a founder director of March Engineering. Rindt still relished his F2 racing, so Chapman's additional sweetener clinched the deal. Ecclestone would run the car under the Jochen Rindt Racing banner.

Goodyear's Leo Mehl recalls the negotiations well: 'Jack was very keen indeed to do this deal because he really did want to retire. I had become quite a good friend of Jochen's and was very keen about the idea, although I feared that money would be the biggest problem. Jochen, Jack and I had talked about it, but nobody really mentioned any hard figures. But Colin Chapman came up to me at one of the races with a very serious look in his eye and whispered, "I don't care how much you are going to offer him, because it won't be enough..." Well, I was young and innocent and Colin was old and forceful, so I never pursued the matter any further with my management.'

Notwithstanding the failure of these talks, Rindt's apprehension about continuing with Lotus could be judged from the fact that, in addition, he not only talked to the fledgling March team, but also tantalised Robin Herd, another of the March founders, with the offer of his own F1 programme. As far as the March deal was concerned, director Max Mosley's determination that the team should push ahead on a broad development front, encompassing the manufacture of production racing cars for several formulae, was not at all to Rindt's liking. Having unsuccessfully attempted to lure Robin Herd away from his three partners, Jochen eventually shied away from the whole idea. 'Absolutely typical of Jochen,' shrugged Alan Rees. 'If he couldn't control the whole deal, then he just didn't want to know...'

For his part, Herd recalls being entertained to dinner in an expensive London restaurant, just off Berkeley Square, where Bernie Ecclestone outlined a proposal from Rindt that the three of them should establish a new company. Rindt and Herd would each take 45 per cent of the share capital, Ecclestone a mere ten per cent. But it never came together.

Mosley, meanwhile, jumped into his Lotus Elan and drove down to Switzerland during the summer of '69 to visit Jochen's home to continue negotiations.

'I don't think he was ever really serious about joining March,' muses Max, 'I just think he needed to convince himself that going with Robin was the right idea. He explained to me why he thought that March would never get off the ground and I explained why I knew it would – and why his project would not. I liked Jochen a lot and had got to know him well when we were all racing F2 together in '68. He was stupendously quick, a phenomenon...'

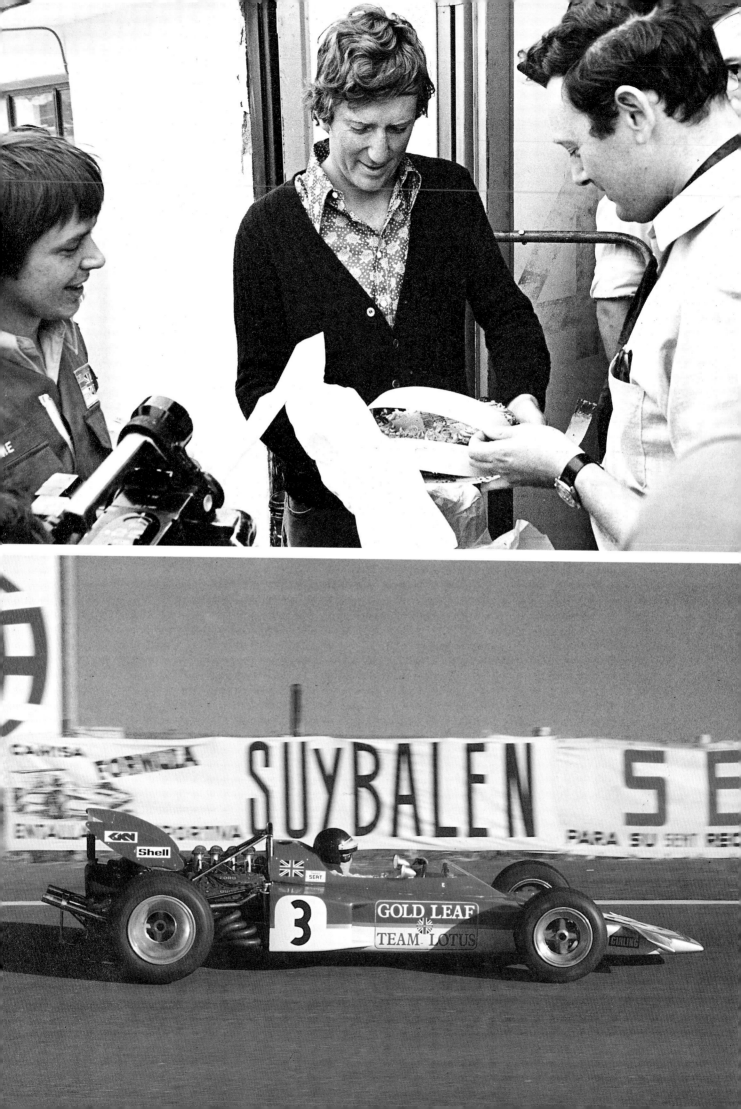

In the 1970 South African Grand Prix at the wheel of the Lotus 49C. Chapman's new secret weapon, the Lotus 72, was not ready by this stage in the season.

For the 1970 season, of course, Chapman had something very special up his sleeve, a piece of equipment which would finally allow Jochen to unlock his World Championship-winning potential. This was the superbly radical Lotus 72, with its rearward weight bias, torsion bar suspension, inboard front disc brakes, side-mounted water radiators and distinctive chisel profile. Just as the type 49 had reasserted the famous British team in the role of Grand Prix pacemakers, so the 72 produced another dramatic quantum leap forward.

Development problems with the new car meant that it wasn't ready for the South African Grand Prix which opened the 1970 season at Kyalami on 7 March, so Jochen and his team-mate John Miles (the son of thespian Sir Bernard Miles, the founder of London's Mermaid Theatre) drove further-uprated Lotus 49s, now revamped to 'C' specification with smaller 13-inch front wheels and revised suspension. Graham Hill had been 'farmed out' to Rob Walker, who was to be supplied with a Lotus 72 by Chapman at a preferential price as part of the deal.

The season began badly for Jochen. At the first corner he tangled with Brabham (ironically) and Chris Amon's new March 701, spinning to a halt on the outfield. He had climbed back to fifth when his engine failed with eight laps to go. The race was won by Brabham, which made Jochen think…

Next on the agenda was the Spanish Grand Prix at Járama, where the Lotus 72 finally arrived on the scene. It was clearly going to need more sorting and, worryingly, during practice a front shaft to one of the inboard disc brakes sheared, pitching Jochen into an abrupt spin. He walked back to the pits and told Chapman he wasn't ever 'going to get into that bloody car again'.

Rob Walker: 'I witnessed this shout-up between Jochen and Colin from our adjacent pit, so I asked Graham, "What happens now?" Of course, Graham was a seasoned Lotus campaigner and he explained, "Colin will put his arm round Rindt's shoulder and lead him away for a friendly little chat … and Jochen will eventually get back into the car." And that's exactly what happened!'

*Jochen's second win with the old Lotus 49 – now to 'C'
specification – came in the 1970 Monaco Grand Prix when
he hustled Jack Brabham's Brabham BT33 (below left)
into a last-corner mistake. Left: Jochen at the Gasometer
hairpin, where he took the lead on the final lap, only yards
from the chequered flag.*

*Celebrating his '70 Monaco victory with the Rainiers – and
looking unexpectedly sombre after that last-corner triumph.*

Jochen lasted only ten laps in the Spanish event and the type 72s were withdrawn from service for further development, obliging the team to field 49Cs in the Monaco Grand Prix. This was to produce one of Rindt's most startling performances, even though his eighth place on the grid and leisurely pace in the early stages of the race fuelled the argument of his critics who said that he was only really hungry for success when he could see a realistic chance of victory.

For much of the 80-lap race Rindt was down around sixth and seventh, apparently taking things easily. At half-distance Brabham was 2.6 seconds ahead of Amon and 15.2 seconds ahead of Rindt. Twenty laps later the gaps were identical, but then Amon dropped out with suspension problems and Jochen got a whiff of the victory rostrum...

With ten laps to go the gap was 11.4 seconds and six laps later Jochen was still nine seconds adrift. Then Brabham was balked by Siffert and the gap shrank to four seconds with three laps to go, Jochen by now piling on the pressure like a man possessed, hurling the Lotus 49C from lock to lock through the Monte Carlo streets.

At the start of the last lap Brabham still had 1.5 seconds in hand, but Rindt must have taken five lengths from him under braking for the chicane last time round. As they sped towards the old Gasworks Hairpin on the final lap, Rindt was close, but not close enough. Then Jack made an error of judgement. Wrong-footed as they came up to lap Piers Courage in the Frank Williams de Tomaso, he locked a wheel and slid straight into the straw bales. Jochen nipped round behind him and won the race!

*Jochen, back in the Lotus 49C, leads Jacky Ickx's Ferrari
312B1 and the Matra of Jean-Pierre Beltoise during the
early stages of the 1970 Belgian Grand Prix.*

He used the Lotus 49C again at Spa-Francorchamps for the Belgian Grand
Prix, starting from the middle of the front row and leading before the engine failed. The winner turned out to be Pedro Rodriguez in the BRM P153, against all odds...

Finally the definitive Lotus 72 made its appearance at Zandvoort in the Dutch Grand
Prix. A suspension redesign had seen many of the anti-squat characteristics – which in
Rindt's view had left the car devoid of 'feel' – removed and Jochen simply trampled the
opposition into the ground to score his second win of the season. And yet it was a joyless triumph for the Austrian.

The entire F1 fraternity was devastated by the death of Piers Courage, whose de
Tomaso crashed in flames on lap 23. Photographs taken on the winner's rostrum show
Rindt barely acknowledging his own success. He looks haunted and tense. Friends say
that this was the beginning of the end of his enthusiasm for Grand Prix racing. Jochen
and Nina had been inseparable from Piers and his wife Sally.

*Rindt's first win with the sensational Lotus 72 came in the
1970 Dutch Grand Prix at Zandvoort – the race in which
Piers Courage was killed.*

Uneasy alliance. Chapman and Rindt knew they needed each other, but it was never a particularly warm or cordial partnership.

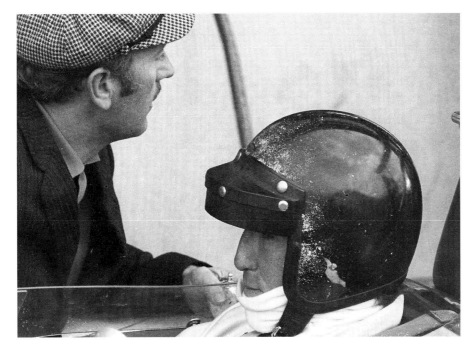

At Clermont-Ferrand for the French Grand Prix, Jochen was regarding the Lotus 72 with increasing, yet arguably justified, paranoia. 'What am I going to do with this bloke?' fumed Chapman to Denis Jenkinson. 'He has lightning reflexes, is bloody quick, but keeps telling me how to design my cars.'

Stewart: 'Jochen certainly didn't get on well with Chapman and definitely did not like the Lotus 72. All through that 1970 season he was worried that it was too fragile. He liked the Lotus 49, of course. It was more his sort of car...'

Stewart's contention is totally endorsed by Rindt's mechanic at the time, Herbie Blash, who, through 1969 and into 1970, saw the Austrian becoming increasingly preoccupied over Chapman's obsession with saving weight and bulk at any cost. Stewart added: 'Colin's whole approach was just a little too slapdash for me, certainly, and that's why I never drove for him. Anyway, by the time of his death I think Jochen was seriously thinking in terms of retirement. He had already become involved in property development, and the Jochen Rindt Show in Vienna had become one of Europe's leading racing car exhibitions. He definitely talked to me about getting out of racing. He told me, "I can't get on with his car ... it's going to break," but he just had to drive it because it was so fast.'

On the personal front, there were rumours that he and Nina were on the verge of splitting up. Yet Jochen had reputedly wagered her $20,000 that he would retire at the end of the season. 'Had he lived, I think they would still have been together today,' grins Jackie, 'still strong willed, still rowing dreadfully...' Others are less convinced.

*Jochen just ahead of Jack Brabham's slowing BT33 in the
'70 British GP at Brands Hatch.*

*Happy man. Jochen with Nina on the victory rostrum
at Brands Hatch after his lucky victory in the 1970
British Grand Prix. The World Championship was
coming closer…*

Despite his misgivings about the 72, Rindt won at Clermont, then again at Brands Hatch, where the British Grand Prix fell into his lap after Brabham ran low on fuel. There was some slight post-race concern that the car might be disqualified due to a problem with the width of its side pods, but this was duly smoothed over.

At Hockenheim, where the German round of the championship had been switched following demands for improved safety facilities at the old Nürburgring, Jochen scored what was to be the final Grand Prix victory of his career. In a tense, slipstreaming battle, he outfumbled Jacky Ickx's Ferrari 312B1 after a gripping contest which saw the two drivers swapping places several times a lap. 'A monkey could have won today in this car. Thank you!' he said to Chapman.

Sadly for his fans, Jochen would not manage to notch up another win in the first World Championship Austrian Grand Prix to be held at the Österreichring; he was running fourth when his Lotus 72's engine failed. Before Monza, there would be an outing in the non-title F1 Oulton Park Gold Cup and a fine heat win at the Salzburgring in his Jochen Rindt Racing F2 Lotus 69. *Motoring News*'s correspondent on the spot, Mike Doodson, remembers this victory giving Rindt particular satisfaction, for he beat Ickx's BMW in a straight fight, even though his retirement in the other heat wrote him out of the aggregate result.

*Jochen leads the sensational four-way battle for the lead
during the opening stages of the first German Grand Prix
to be held at Hockenheim. The Ferraris of Jacky Ickx and
Clay Regazzoni and Chris Amon's March are hanging
on in his slipstream.*

Last photograph. Jochen with his Lotus 72, shorn of rear wing and nose spoilers, a matter of minutes before his fatal accident during final qualifying for the Italian Grand Prix, 5 September 1970.

On Saturday 5 September 1970 Jochen Rindt went out to practise in his Lotus 72 at Monza in preparation for the Italian Grand Prix. At Chapman's insistence, he was running without nose wings or aerofoil in an attempt to squeeze out of it as much straightline speed as possible to counter the more powerful flat-12 Ferraris. Rindt's team-mate John Miles was told that he had to do the same, but was adamant that the car felt horrifyingly unstable in this configuration.

Braking hard for Parabolica, Rindt had just overtaken Denny Hulme's McLaren when his 72 began weaving under braking and speared off to the left, impacting very heavily against the inadequately secured guard rail. The front of the car was torn off as the Lotus's chisel nose jammed under the barrier and Jochen, who never secured the crotch straps on his six-point harness, was plunged into the cockpit, severing his jugular vein on its main buckle.

There seems little doubt that Rindt succumbed almost immediately, although Italian legal protocol dictated – officially – that he died in the sordid confines of an ambulance taking him to Milan's Niguarda clinic. A lengthy investigation eventually attributed Jochen's loss of control to the fracturing of one of those front brakeshafts, although aerodynamic instability on cold tyres was also a significant factor.

A few days later, Jochen was buried in his home town of Graz. Yet not until Emerson Fittipaldi won the United States Grand Prix – his fourth-ever F1 race – in a Lotus 72 would Jochen become the sport's first, and so far only, posthumous World Champion. He never lived to know that his supreme, all-pervading ambition had been realised...

'What made it all so sad', reflects Alan Rees, 'is that I think Jochen was just on the point of being recognised for the brilliant top-line driver he really was. I think he would have raced for a few more years – not for long, mind you – and then people would have realised that he was right up there with Jim Clark in terms of pure talent and speed.'

POSTSCRIPT

Many of the principal supporting players in the Jochen Rindt story are still alive, some not. Nina has been married twice since Jochen's death, first to international gambler Philip Martyn, more recently to Alex, Viscount Bridport. She still lives in Switzerland. Jochen's daughter Natascha is now 22, and an accomplished skier like her father. She spent one recent summer training intensively with the Austrian national ski team on snowy glaciers, but has since shelved her early ambition to become a ski racer.

Colin Chapman died in December 1982 of a sudden heart attack. Sir Jack Brabham is retired, while Ron Tauranac runs his own company, Ralt, now part of the March Group. Bernie Ecclestone has become the single most influential figure in Grand Prix racing. When asked to recall Jochen, he just shrugs: 'What can I say? Just a super, straightforward bloke. The fastest driver of his era.'

Jackie Stewart, safely retired from the sport for almost two decades, still lives with Helen at Clayton House, Begnins, just up the road from his late friend's Swiss home. Herbie Blash is team manager of Brabham, treasuring memories of 'that fabulous guy' he worked for in 1969 and '70. John Judd now builds Grand Prix engines of his own. Helmut Marko currently runs a Mercedes saloon car racing team and fields a Formula 3000 car for the latest Austrian rising star, Karl Wendlinger. Marko's hopes of following Jochen to a front-line Grand Prix career ended when he was blinded in one eye by a flying rock at the wheel of a BRM in the 1972 French Grand Prix at Clermont-Ferrand.

Denis Jenkinson, 70 this year, still writes as trenchantly for *Motor Sport* magazine as he did in Rindt's heyday. Leo Mehl has since been promoted to the exalted status of Goodyear's International Director of Racing. Alan Rees is team manager and a director of the Footwork Arrows F1 team, and Frank Williams, paralysed in a road accident in 1986, now presides over one of Britain's leading Grand Prix constructors.

Heinz Prüller, Rindt's close friend and biographer, still commentates enthusiastically on Formula 1 for Austrian Television. He has supported the careers of Helmut Marko, Niki Lauda and Gerhard Berger with the same unbridled, vociferous and patriotic enthusiasm that he once reserved for Jochen...

JOCHEN RINDT · CAREER RECORD
(1964–1970)
BY JOHN TAYLOR

1964

	Race	Circuit	Date	Entrant	Car	Comment
12/ret	Prix von Wien–Heat 1	Aspern	12/04/64	Ford Austria	Brabham BT10-Cosworth SCA	
ret	Prix von Wien–Heat 2	Aspern	12/04/64	Ford Austria	Brabham BT10-Cosworth SCA	
nc	Prix von Wien–Aggregate	Aspern	12/04/64	Ford Austria	Brabham BT10-Cosworth SCA	
4	ADAC Eifelrennen	Nürburgring	26/04/64	Ford Austria	Brabham BT10-Cosworth SCA	
3	Grovewood Trophy	Mallory Park	17/05/64	Ford Austria	Brabham BT10-Cosworth SCA	Pole
1	London Trophy–Heat 2	Crystal Palace	18/05/64	Ford Austria	Brabham BT10-Cosworth SCA	
1	London Trophy–Final	Crystal Palace	18/05/64	Ford Austria	Brabham BT10-Cosworth SCA	Fastest lap
ret	Preis von Berlin–Heat 1	Avus	24/05/64	Ford Austria	Brabham BT10-Cosworth SCA	suspension
ret	Le Mans 24 Hours	Le Mans	20–21/06/64	David Piper	Ferrari 275LM	oil filter/c/d Piper
ret	Grand Prix de Reims	Reims	05/07/64	Ford Austria	Brabham BT10-Cosworth SCA	accident
3	Trophée d'Auvergne	Clermont-Ferrand	19/07/64	Ford Austria	Brabham BT10-Cosworth SCA	
6	British Eagle Trophy	Brands Hatch	03/08/64	Ford Austria	Brabham BT10-Cosworth SCA	
ret	AUSTRIAN GP	Zeltweg	23/08/64	R.R.C.Walker Racing Team	Brabham BT11-BRM	steering
ret	Grand Prix d'Albi	Albi	13/09/64	Ford Austria	Brabham BT10-Cosworth SCA	battery
ret	Gold Cup	Oulton Park	19/09/64	Ford Austria	Brabham BT10-Cosworth SCA	clutch
ret	Grand Prix d'Ile de France	Montlhéry	27/09/64	Ford Austria	Brabham BT10-Cosworth SCA	suspension

1965

	Race	Circuit	Date	Entrant	Car	Comment
ret	SOUTH AFRICAN GP	East London	01/01/65	Cooper Car Co.	Cooper T73-Climax FWMV	transistor
13	Daily Mail Race of Champions–Heat 1	Brands Hatch	13/03/65	Cooper Car Co.	Cooper T77-Climax FWMV	
7	Daily Mail Race of Champions–Heat 2	Brands Hatch	13/03/65	Cooper Car Co.	Cooper T77-Climax FWMV	
7	Daily Mail Race of Champions–Aggregate	Brands Hatch	13/03/65	Cooper Car Co.	Cooper T77-Climax FWMV	
ret	Daily Express Trophy	Oulton Park	03/04/65	Roy Winkelmann Racing	Brabham BT16-Cosworth SCA	gearbox/Fastest lap
18	Autocar Trophy–Heat 1	Snetterton	10/04/65	Roy Winkelmann Racing	Brabham BT16-Cosworth SCA	Pole
ret	Autocar Trophy–Heat 2	Snetterton	10/04/65	Roy Winkelmann Racing	Brabham BT16-Cosworth SCA	
nc	Autocar Trophy–Aggregate	Snetterton	10/04/65	Roy Winkelmann Racing	Brabham BT16-Cosworth SCA	
dsq	Sunday Mirror Trophy	Goodwood	19/04/65	Cooper Car Co.	Cooper T77-Climax FWMV	missed chicane
3	Grand Prix de Pau	Pau	25/04/65	Roy Winkelmann Racing	Brabham BT16-Cosworth SCA	
ret	BRDC International Trophy	Silverstone	15/05/65	Cooper Car Co.	Cooper T77-Climax FWMV	engine
3	Gran Premio di Roma–Heat 1	Vallelunga	16/05/65	Roy Winkelmann Racing	Brabham BT16-Cosworth SCA	
3	Gran Premio di Roma–Heat 2	Vallelunga	16/05/65	Roy Winkelmann Racing	Brabham BT16-Cosworth SCA	
3	Gran Premio di Roma–Aggregate	Vallelunga	16/05/65	Roy Winkelmann Racing	Brabham BT16-Cosworth SCA	
3	Nürburgring 1000 Km	Nürburgring	23/05/65	Porsche System Engineering	Porsche Carrera 8	c/d Bonnier
dnq	MONACO GP	Monte Carlo	30/05/65	Cooper Car Co.	Cooper T77-Climax FWMV	
4	London Trophy–Heat 1	Crystal Palace	07/06/65	Roy Winkelmann Racing	Brabham BT16-Cosworth SCA	
4	London Trophy–Heat 2	Crystal Palace	07/06/65	Roy Winkelmann Racing	Brabham BT16-Cosworth SCA	
4	London Trophy–Aggregate	Crystal Palace	07/06/65	Roy Winkelmann Racing	Brabham BT16-Cosworth SCA	
11	BELGIAN GP	Spa	13/06/65	Cooper Car Co.	Cooper T77-Climax FWMV	
1	Le Mans 24 Hours	Le Mans	19–20/06/65	North American Racing Team	Ferrari 275LM	c/d Gregory
ret	FRENCH GP	Clermont-Ferrand	27/06/65	Cooper Car Co.	Cooper T77-Climax FWMV	collision with Amon
1	Grand Prix de Reims	Reims	04/07/65	Roy Winkelmann Racing	Brabham BT16-Cosworth SCA	Pole/Fastest lap
14/ret	BRITISH GP	Silverstone	10/07/65	Cooper Car Co.	Cooper T77-Climax FWMV	engine
ret	DUTCH GP	Zandvoort	18/07/65	Cooper Car Co.	Cooper T77-Climax FWMV	oil pressure
4	GERMAN GP	Nürburgring	01/08/65	Cooper Car Co.	Cooper T77-Climax FWMV	
1	Gran Premio di Pergusa-Heat 1	Enna	08/08/65	Roy Winkelmann Racing	Brabham BT16-Cosworth SCA	
2	Gran Premio di Pergusa-Final	Enna	08/08/65	Roy Winkelmann Racing	Brabham BT16-Cosworth SCA	
ret	F1 Gran Premio di Mediterraneo	Enna	15/08/65	Roy Winkelmann Racing	Brabham BT16-Cosworth SCA	driveshaft/F2 car
1	Austrian Grand Prix	Zeltweg	22/08/65	Gotfrid Köchert	Ferrari 275LM	
8	ITALIAN GP	Monza	12/09/65	Cooper Car Co.	Cooper T77-Climax FWMV	
ret	Gold Cup	Oulton Park	18/09/65	Roy Winkelmann Racing	Brabham BT16-Cosworth SCA	driveshaft
4	Grand Prix d'Albi	Albi	26/09/65	Roy Winkelmann Racing	Brabham BT16-Cosworth SCA	
6	US GP	Watkins Glen	03/10/65	Cooper Car Co.	Cooper T77-Climax FWMV	
ret	MEXICAN GP	Mexico City	24/10/65	Cooper Car Co.	Cooper T77-Climax FWMV	ignition

1966

	Race	Circuit	Date	Entrant	Car	Comment
1	4-Hour Trans-Am Saloon Car Race	Sebring	25/03/66	Autodelta	Alfa Romeo GTA	
3	Sunday Mirror Trophy	Goodwood	11/04/66	Roy Winkelmann Racing	Brabham BT18-Cosworth SCA	
ret	Grand Prix de Pau	Pau	17/04/66	Roy Winkelmann Racing	Brabham BT18-Cosworth SCA	engine–crashed
1	ADAC Eifelrennen	Nürburgring	24/04/66	Roy Winkelmann Racing	Brabham BT18-Cosworth SCA	Pole/Fastest lap
3	Grote Preis van Limborg–Heat 1	Zolder	08/05/66	Roy Winkelmann Racing	Brabham BT18-Cosworth SCA	
3	Grote Preis van Limborg–Heat 2	Zolder	08/05/66	Roy Winkelmann Racing	Brabham BT18-Cosworth SCA	
3	Grote Preis van Limborg–Aggregate	Zolder	08/05/66	Roy Winkelmann Racing	Brabham BT18-Cosworth SCA	
5	International Trophy	Silverstone	14/05/66	Cooper Car Co.	Cooper T81-Maserati	
ret	MONACO GP	Monte Carlo	22/05/66	Cooper Car Co.	Cooper T81-Maserati	engine

1966 (continued)

4	London Trophy–Heat 1	Crystal Palace	30/05/66	Roy Winkelmann Racing	Brabham BT18-Cosworth SCA	
4	London Trophy–Heat 2	Crystal Palace	30/05/66	Roy Winkelmann Racing	Brabham BT18-Cosworth SCA	
4	London Trophy–Aggregate	Crystal Palace	30/05/66	Roy Winkelmann Racing	Brabham BT18-Cosworth SCA	
ret	Nürburgring 1000 Km	Nürburgring	06/06/66	Porsche System Engineering	Porsche Carrera P8	*brakes/c/d Vaccarella*
2	BELGIAN GP	Spa	13/06/66	Cooper Car Co.	Cooper T81-Maserati	
ret	Le Mans 24 Hours	Le Mans	18–19/06/66	F. English Ltd	Ford GT40	*engine/c/d Ireland*
ret	Grand Prix de Reims	Reims	02/07/66	Roy Winkelmann Racing	Brabham BT18-Cosworth SCA	*boiling fuel*
4	FRENCH GP	Reims	03/07/66	Cooper Car Co.	Cooper T81-Maserati	
ret	Grand Prix de Rouen	Rouen	10/07/66	Roy Winkelmann Racing	Brabham BT18-Cosworth SCA	*gearbox*
5	BRITISH GP	Brands Hatch	16/07/66	Cooper Car Co.	Cooper T81-Maserati	
ret	DUTCH GP	Zandvoort	24/07/66	Cooper Car Co.	Cooper T81-Maserati	*accident*
ret	Snetterton 500 Km	Snetterton	30/07/66	Autodelta	Alfa Romeo GTA	*spun off*
3	GERMAN GP	Nürburgring	07/08/66	Cooper Car Co.	Cooper T81-Maserati	
ret	Kanonloppet	Karlskoga	21/08/66	Roy Winkelmann Racing	Brabham BT18-Cosworth SCA	*hit Offenstadt*
4	Suomen Grand Prix–Heat 1	Keimola	24/08/66	Roy Winkelmann Racing	Brabham BT18-Cosworth SCA	
4	Suomen Grand Prix–Heat 2	Keimola	24/08/66	Roy Winkelmann Racing	Brabham BT18-Cosworth SCA	
4	Suomen Grand Prix–Aggregate	Keimola	24/08/66	Roy Winkelmann Racing	Brabham BT18-Cosworth SCA	
4	ITALIAN GP	Monza	04/09/66	Cooper Car Co.	Cooper T81-Maserati	
9	Austrian Grand Prix	Zeltweg	11/09/66	Col. Ronnie Hoare	Ford GT40	
ret	Trophée Craven 'A'	Le Mans	18/09/66	Roy Winkelmann Racing	Brabham BT18-Cosworth SCA	*throttle*
ret	Grand Prix d'Albi	Albi	25/09/66	Roy Winkelmann Racing	Brabham BT18-Cosworth SCA	*engine*
2	US GP	Watkins Glen	02/10/66	Cooper Car Co.	Cooper T81-Maserati	
2	Prix du Tyrol	Innsbruck	09/10/66	Porsche System Engineering	Porsche Carrera 6	*Fastest lap*
1	Innsbruck Saloon Car Race	Innsbruck	09/10/66	Autodelta	Alfa Romeo GTA	
2	Donaupokal Sports Car Race	Aspern	16/10/66	Porsche System Engineering	Porsche Carrera 6	*Pole*
ret	Donaupokal Saloon Car Race	Aspern	16/10/66	Autodelta	Alfa Romeo GTA	*gear lever*
ret	MEXICAN GP	Mexico City	23/10/66	Cooper Car Co.	Cooper T81-Maserati	*wishbone*
1	Motor Show 200–Heat 1	Brands Hatch	30/10/66	Roy Winkelmann Racing	Brabham BT18-Cosworth SCA	*Pole*
1	Motor Show 200–Final	Brands Hatch	30/10/66	Roy Winkelmann Racing	Brabham BT18-Cosworth SCA	*Pole/Fastest lap*

1967

ret	SOUTH AFRICAN GP	Kyalami	02/01/67	Cooper Car Co.	Cooper T81-Maserati	*engine*
ret	Daytona Continental 24 Hours	Daytona	04–05/02/67	Porsche System Engineering	Porsche Carrera 6	*suspension/c/d Mitter*
18	Race of Champions–Heat 1	Brands Hatch	12/03/67	Cooper Car Co.	Cooper T81-Maserati	
ret	Race of Champions–Final	Brands Hatch	12/03/67	Cooper Car Co.	Cooper T81-Maserati	*steering/gearbox*
1	Guards One Hundred–Heat 1	Snetterton	24/03/67	Roy Winkelmann Racing	Brabham BT23-Cosworth FVA	*Pole*
ret	Guards One Hundred–Heat 2	Snetterton	24/03/67	Roy Winkelmann Racing	Brabham BT23-Cosworth FVA	*electrics/Pole*
1	Guards One Hundred–Final	Snetterton	24/03/67	Roy Winkelmann Racing	Brabham BT23-Cosworth FVA	*Pole/Fastest lap*
1	Wills Trophy–Heat 1	Silverstone	27/03/67	Roy Winkelmann Racing	Brabham BT23-Cosworth FVA	*Pole/Fastest lap*
1	Wills Trophy–Heat 2	Silverstone	27/03/67	Roy Winkelmann Racing	Brabham BT23-Cosworth FVA	*Pole/Fastest lap*
1	Wills Trophy–Aggregate	Silverstone	27/03/67	Roy Winkelmann Racing	Brabham BT23-Cosworth FVA	
1	Grand Prix de Pau	Pau	02/04/67	Roy Winkelmann Racing	Brabham BT23-Cosworth FVA	
2	Gran Premio Barcelona	Montjuich Park	09/04/67	Roy Winkelmann Racing	Brabham BT23-Cosworth FVA	*Fastest lap*
1	ADAC Eifelrennen	Nürburgring	23/04/67	Roy Winkelmann Racing	Brabham BT23-Cosworth FVA	
3	Monza 1000 Km	Monza	30/04/67	Porsche System Engineering	Porsche 910	*c/d Mitter*
ret	MONACO GP	Monte Carlo	07/05/67	Cooper Car Co.	Cooper T81B-Maserati	*gearbox*
24/ret	Indianapolis 500	Indianapolis	30–31/05/67	All American Racers	Eagle-Gurney Weslake Ford	*flooded engine*
ret	DUTCH GP	Zandvoort	04/06/67	Cooper Car Co.	Cooper T81B-Maserati	*suspension*
ret	Le Mans 24 Hours	Le Mans	10–11/06/67	Porsche System Engineering	Porsche 907	*engine/c/d Mitter*
4	BELGIAN GP	Spa	18/06/67	Cooper Car Co.	Cooper T81B-Maserati	
1	Trophées de France	Reims	25/06/67	Roy Winkelmann Racing	Brabham BT23-Cosworth FVA	
ret	FRENCH GP	Le Mans	02/07/67	Cooper Car Co.	Cooper T81B-Maserati	*engine*
1	Trophées de France	Rouen	09/07/67	Roy Winkelmann Racing	Brabham BT23-Cosworth FVA	*Pole/Fastest lap*
ret	BRITISH GP	Silverstone	15/07/67	Cooper Car Co.	Cooper T86-Maserati	*gearbox*
1	Internationales Flugplatzrennen	Tulln-Langenlebarn	16/07/67	Roy Winkelmann Racing	Brabham BT23-Cosworth FVA	
ret	Gran Premio de Madrid	Járama	23/07/67	Roy Winkelmann Racing	Brabham BT23-Cosworth FVA	*puncture*
11	BOAC 500	Brands Hatch	30/07/67	Porsche System Engineering	Porsche 910	*c/d Schütz*
ret	GERMAN GP	Nürburgring	06/08/67	Cooper Car Co.	Cooper T86-Maserati	*engine*
2	Kanonloppet	Karlskoga	13/08/67	Roy Winkelmann Racing	Brabham BT23-Cosworth FVA	*Pole/Fastest lap*
10	Austrian Grand Prix	Zeltweg	20/08/67	Porsche System Engineering	Porsche Carrera 6	*c/d Stommelen*
ret	CANADIAN GP	Mosport Park	27/08/67	Cooper Car Co.	Cooper T86-Maserati	*ignition*
1	Guards International Trophy–Heat 1	Brands Hatch	28/08/67	Roy Winkelmann Racing	Brabham BT23-Cosworth FVA	*Pole/Fastest lap*
1	Guards International Trophy–Final	Brands Hatch	28/08/67	Roy Winkelmann Racing	Brabham BT23-Cosworth FVA	*Pole/Fastest lap*
2	Suomen Grand Prix–Qualifying Heat	Keimola	03/09/67	Roy Winkelmann Racing	Brabham BT23-Cosworth FVA	*Pole*
2	Suomen Grand Prix–Final	Keimola	03/09/67	Roy Winkelmann Racing	Brabham BT23-Cosworth FVA	
1	Hämeenlinna Ajot	Hämeenlinna	05/09/67	Roy Winkelmann Racing	Brabham BT23-Cosworth FVA	
4	ITALIAN GP	Monza	10/09/67	Cooper Car Co.	Cooper T86-Maserati	
7	Gold Cup	Oulton Park	17/09/67	Roy Winkelmann Racing	Brabham BT23-Cosworth FVA	*5th F2 class*
2	Grand Prix d'Albi	Albi	24/09/67	Roy Winkelmann Racing	Brabham BT23-Cosworth FVA	
ret	US GP	Watkins Glen	01/10/67	Cooper Car Co.	Cooper T86-Maserati	*engine*

1968

Pos	Race	Circuit	Date	Entrant	Car	Notes
3	SOUTH AFRICAN GP	Kyalami	01/01/68	Brabham Racing Organisation	Brabham BT24-Repco	
11/ret	Gran Premio Barcelona	Montjuich Park	31/03/68	Roy Winkelmann Racing	Brabham BT23C-Cosworth FVA	fuel line
1	BARC Thruxton Trophy–Heat 2	Thruxton	15/04/68	Roy Winkelmann Racing	Brabham BT23C-Cosworth FVA	Pole/Fastest lap
1	BARC Thruxton Trophy–Final	Thruxton	15/04/68	Roy Winkelmann Racing	Brabham BT23C-Cosworth FVA	Pole/Fastest lap
ret	Grand Prix de Pau	Pau	21/04/68	Roy Winkelmann Racing	Brabham BT23C-Cosworth FVA	radiator hose/Pole
2	Gran Premio de Madrid	Járama	28/04/68	Roy Winkelmann Racing	Brabham BT23C-Cosworth FVA	Pole
1	Grand Prix du Limborg–Heat 1	Zolder	05/05/68	Roy Winkelmann Racing	Brabham BT23C-Cosworth FVA	Pole/Fastest lap
3	Grand Prix du Limborg–Heat 2	Zolder	05/05/68	Roy Winkelmann Racing	Brabham BT23C-Cosworth FVA	Pole/Fastest lap
1	Grand Prix du Limborg–Aggregate	Zolder	05/05/68	Roy Winkelmann Racing	Brabham BT23C-Cosworth FVA	
ret	SPANISH GP	Járama	12/05/68	Brabham Racing Organisation	Brabham BT24-Repco	overheating
ret	MONACO GP	Monte Carlo	26/05/68	Brabham Racing Organisation	Brabham BT24-Repco	spun off
32/ret	Indianapolis 500	Indianapolis	30/05/68	Brabham Racing Organisation	Brabham BT25-Repco	engine
1	Holts Trophy–Heat 1	Crystal Palace	03/06/68	Roy Winkelmann Racing	Brabham BT23C-Cosworth FVA	
1	Holts Trophy–Final	Crystal Palace	03/06/68	Roy Winkelmann Racing	Brabham BT23C-Cosworth FVA	Fastest lap
ret	BELGIAN GP	Spa	09/06/68	Brabham Racing Organisation	Brabham BT26-Repco	Pole/Fastest lap
1	Rhine Cup	Hockenheim	16/06/68	Roy Winkelmann Racing	Brabham BT23C-Cosworth FVA	engine
ret	DUTCH GP	Zandvoort	23/06/68	Brabham Racing Organisation	Brabham BT26-Repco	Fastest lap
ret	FRENCH GP	Rouen	07/07/68	Brabham Racing Organisation	Brabham BT26-Repco	ignition/battery
1	OAMTC Flugplatzrennen–Heat 1	Tulln-Langenlebarn	14/07/68	Roy Winkelmann Racing	Brabham BT23C-Cosworth FVA	fuel leak/Pole
1	OAMTC Flugplatzrennen–Heat 2	Tulln-Langenlebarn	14/07/68	Roy Winkelmann Racing	Brabham BT23C-Cosworth FVA	Pole/Fastest lap
1	OAMTC Flugplatzrennen–Aggregate	Tulln-Langenlebarn	14/07/68	Roy Winkelmann Racing	Brabham BT23C-Cosworth FVA	Pole/Fastest lap
ret	BRITISH GP	Brands Hatch	20/07/68	Brabham Racing Organisation	Brabham BT26-Repco	
3	GERMAN GP	Nürburgring	04/08/68	Brabham Racing Organisation	Brabham BT26-Repco	electrics
ret	Gold Cup	Oulton Park	17/08/68	Brabham Racing Organisation	Brabham BT26-Repco	
1	Gran Premio del Mediterraneo	Enna	25/08/68	Roy Winkelmann Racing	Brabham BT23C-Cosworth FVA	oil seal
ret	ITALIAN GP	Monza	08/09/68	Brabham Racing Organisation	Brabham BT26-Repco	Fastest lap
ret	Trophées de France	Reims	15/09/68	Roy Winkelmann Racing	Brabham BT23C-Cosworth FVA	engine
ret	CANADIAN GP	St Jovite	22/09/68	Brabham Racing Organisation	Brabham BT26-Repco	fuel pipe/Pole
ret	US GP	Watkins Glen	06/10/68	Brabham Racing Organisation	Brabham BT26-Repco	overheating/Pole
14/ret	Preis von Württemberg	Hockenheim	13/10/68	Roy Winkelmann Racing	Brabham BT23C-Cosworth FVA	engine
11/ret	Grand Prix d'Albi	Albi	20/10/68	Roy Winkelmann Racing	Brabham BT23C-Cosworth FVA	vibration/Pole
ret	MEXICAN GP	Mexico City	03/11/68	Brabham Racing Organisation	Brabham BT26-Repco	ignition/Pole/Fastest lap
ret	Temporada Series, round 1	Buenos Aires	01/12/68	Roy Winkelmann Racing	Brabham BT23C-Cosworth FVA	ignition
2	Temporada Series, round 2	Cordoba	08/12/68	Roy Winkelmann Racing	Brabham BT23C-Cosworth FVA	wing/Pole
3	Temporada Series, round 3	San Juan	15/12/68	Roy Winkelmann Racing	Brabham BT23C-Cosworth FVA	Fastest lap
2	Temporada Series, round 4	Buenos Aires	22/12/68	Roy Winkelmann Racing	Brabham BT23C-Cosworth FVA	

1969

Pos	Race	Circuit	Date	Entrant	Car	Notes
2	New Zealand Grand Prix	Pukekohe	04/01/69	Gold Leaf Team Lotus	Lotus 49T-Cosworth DFW	Fastest lap
4	Rothmans International–Heat 1	Levin	11/01/69	Gold Leaf Team Lotus	Lotus 49T-Cosworth DFW	Pole/Fastest lap
ret	Rothmans International–Final	Levin	11/01/69	Gold Leaf Team Lotus	Lotus 49T-Cosworth DFW	accident/Fastest lap
2	Lady Wigram Trophy–Heat 2	Christchurch	18/01/69	Gold Leaf Team Lotus	Lotus 49B-Cosworth DFW	Pole
1	Lady Wigram Trophy–Final	Christchurch	18/01/69	Gold Leaf Team Lotus	Lotus 49B-Cosworth DFW	Pole/Fastest lap
1	Rothmans International–Heat 1	Invercargill	25/01/69	Gold Leaf Team Lotus	Lotus 49B-Cosworth DFW	Pole/Fastest lap
ret	Rothmans International–Final	Invercargill	25/01/69	Gold Leaf Team Lotus	Lotus 49B-Cosworth DFW	driveshaft/Pole
ret	Australian Grand Prix	Lakeside	02/02/69	Gold Leaf Team Lotus	Lotus 49B-Cosworth DFW	engine
1	Tasman International 100	Warwick Farm	09/02/69	Gold Leaf Team Lotus	Lotus 49B-Cosworth DFW	Pole
2	Sandown Park International	Sandown Park	16/02/69	Gold Leaf Team Lotus	Lotus 49B-Cosworth DFW	Pole
ret	SOUTH AFRICAN GP	Kyalami	01/03/69	Gold Leaf Team Lotus	Lotus 49B-Cosworth DFV	fuel pump
ret	Race of Champions	Brands Hatch	16/03/69	Gold Leaf Team Lotus	Lotus 49B-Cosworth DFV	oil pressure/Fastest lap
2	Daily Express International Trophy	Silverstone	30/03/69	Gold Leaf Team Lotus	Lotus 49B-Cosworth DFV	Fastest lap
13	Wills Trophy–Heat 2	Thruxton	07/04/69	Roy Winkelmann Racing	Lotus 59-Cosworth FVA	puncture/Pole/Fastest lap
1	Wills Trophy–Final	Thruxton	07/04/69	Roy Winkelmann Racing	Lotus 59-Cosworth FVA	Fastest lap
1	Grand Prix de Pau	Pau	20/04/69	Roy Winkelmann Racing	Lotus 59B-Cosworth FVA	Pole/Fastest lap
ret	ADAC Eifelrennen	Nürburgring	27/04/69	Roy Winkelmann Racing	Lotus 59B-Cosworth FVA	wishbone
ret	SPANISH GP	Montjuich Park	04/05/69	Gold Leaf Team Lotus	Lotus 49B-Cosworth DFV	accident/Pole/Fastest lap
1	Grand Prix du Limborg–Heat 1	Zolder	08/06/69	Roy Winkelmann Racing	Lotus 59B-Cosworth FVA	
1	Grand Prix du Limborg–Heat 2	Zolder	08/06/69	Roy Winkelmann Racing	Lotus 59B-Cosworth FVA	Pole
1	Grand Prix du Limborg–Aggregate	Zolder	08/06/69	Roy Winkelmann Racing	Lotus 59B-Cosworth FVA	
ret	DUTCH GP	Zandvoort	21/06/69	Gold Leaf Team Lotus	Lotus 49B-Cosworth DFV	driveshaft/Pole
ret	FRENCH GP	Clermont-Ferrand	06/07/69	Gold Leaf Team Lotus	Lotus 49B-Cosworth DFV	sick
1	OAMTC Flugplatzrennen–Heat 1	Tulln-Langenlebarn	13/07/69	Roy Winkelmann Racing	Lotus 59B-Cosworth FVA	Pole/Fastest lap
1	OAMTC Flugplatzrennen–Heat 2	Tulln-Langenlebarn	13/07/69	Roy Winkelmann Racing	Lotus 59B-Cosworth FVA	Pole/Fastest lap
1	OAMTC Flugplatzrennen–Aggregate	Tulln-Langenlebarn	13/07/69	Roy Winkelmann Racing	Lotus 59B-Cosworth FVA	
4	BRITISH GP	Silverstone	19/07/69	Gold Leaf Team Lotus	Lotus 49B-Cosworth DFV	pit stops/Pole
ret	GERMAN GP	Nürburgring	03/08/69	Gold Leaf Team Lotus	Lotus 49B-Cosworth DFV	ignition
2	Gold Cup	Oulton Park	16/08/69	Gold Leaf Team Lotus	Lotus 63-Cosworth DFV	

1969 (continued)

1	Nordic Cup	Keimola	24/08/69	Alex Soler-Roig	Porsche 908	*Pole/Fastest lap*
2	ITALIAN GP	Monza	07/09/69	Gold Leaf Team Lotus	Lotus 49B-Cosworth DFV	*Pole*
3	Grand Prix d'Albi	Albi	14/09/69	Roy Winkelmann Racing	Lotus 59B-Cosworth FVA	*Pole/Fastest lap*
3	CANADIAN GP	Mosport Park	20/09/69	Gold Leaf Team Lotus	Lotus 49B-Cosworth DFV	
1	US GP	Watkins Glen	05/10/69	Gold Leaf Team Lotus	Lotus 49B-Cosworth DFV	*Pole/Fastest lap*
ret	Gran Premio di Roma–Heat 1	Vallelunga	12/10/69	Roy Winkelmann Racing	Lotus 59B-Cosworth FVA	*lost brakes–accident*
ret	MEXICAN GP	Mexico City	19/10/69	Gold Leaf Team Lotus	Lotus 49B-Cosworth DFV	*wishbone*
1	Madrid 6 Hours	Járama	26/10/69	Alex Soler-Roig	Porsche 908	*Pole/Fastest lap/c/d Soler-Roig*

1970

2	Buenos Aires 1000 Km	Buenos Aires	11/01/70	Alex Soler-Roig	Porsche 908	*c/d Soler-Roig*
13/*ret*	SOUTH AFRICAN GP	Kyalami	07/03/70	Gold Leaf Team Lotus	Lotus 49C-Cosworth DFV	*engine*
2	Race of Champions	Brands Hatch	22/03/70	Gold Leaf Team Lotus	Lotus 49C-Cosworth DFV	
1	Wills Trophy–Heat 2	Thruxton	30/03/70	Jochen Rindt Team Lotus	Lotus 69-Cosworth FVA	*Pole/Fastest lap*
1	Wills Trophy–Final	Thruxton	30/03/70	Jochen Rindt Team Lotus	Lotus 69-Cosworth FVA	*Pole/Fastest lap*
1	Grand Prix de Pau	Pau	05/04/70	Jochen Rindt Team Lotus	Lotus 69-Cosworth FVA	*Pole/Fastest lap*
ret	Deutschland Trophäe	Hockenheim	12/04/70	Jochen Rindt Team Lotus	Lotus 69-Cosworth FVA	*accident damage/Pole*
ret	SPANISH GP	Járama	19/04/70	Gold Leaf Team Lotus	Lotus 72-Cosworth DFV	*engine*
5	International Trophy–Heat 1	Silverstone	26/04/70	Gold Leaf Team Lotus	Lotus 72-Cosworth DFV	
ret	International Trophy–Heat 2	Silverstone	26/04/70	Gold Leaf Team Lotus	Lotus 72-Cosworth DFV	*ignition*
nc	International Trophy–Aggregate	Silverstone	26/04/70	Gold Leaf Team Lotus	Lotus 72-Cosworth DFV	
1	ADAC Eifelrennen	Nürburgring	03/05/70	Jochen Rindt Team Lotus	Lotus 69-Cosworth FVA	*Pole/Fastest lap*
1	MONACO GP	Monte Carlo	10/05/70	Gold Leaf Team Lotus	Lotus 49C-Cosworth DFV	*Fastest lap*
1	Grote Preis van Limborg–Heat 1	Zolder	24/05/70	Jochen Rindt Team Lotus	Lotus 69-Cosworth FVA	*Pole/Fastest lap*
1	Grote Preis van Limborg–Heat 2	Zolder	24/05/70	Jochen Rindt Team Lotus	Lotus 69-Cosworth FVA	*Pole/Fastest lap*
1	Grote Preis van Limborg–Aggregate	Zolder	24/05/70	Jochen Rindt Team Lotus	Lotus 69-Cosworth FVA	
1	Alcoa Trophy–Heat 2	Crystal Palace	25/05/70	Jochen Rindt Team Lotus	Lotus 69-Cosworth FVA	*Pole/Fastest lap*
ret	Alcoa Trophy–Final	Crystal Palace	25/05/70	Jochen Rindt Team Lotus	Lotus 69-Cosworth FVA	*battery lead/Pole*
ret	BELGIAN GP	Spa	07/06/70	Gold Leaf Team Lotus	Lotus 49C-Cosworth DFV	*engine*
dns				Gold Leaf Team Lotus	Lotus 72-Cosworth DFV	*practice only*
ret	Rhine Cup	Hockenheim	14/06/70	Jochen Rindt Team Lotus	Lotus 69-Cosworth FVA	*mechanical*
1	DUTCH GP	Zandvoort	21/06/70	Gold Leaf Team Lotus	Lotus 72-Cosworth DFV	*Pole*
2	Grand Prix de Rouen–Heat 2	Rouen	28/06/70	Jochen Rindt Team Lotus	Lotus 69-Cosworth FVA	
9	Grand Prix de Rouen–Final	Rouen	28/06/70	Jochen Rindt Team Lotus	Lotus 69-Cosworth FVA	*engine problems*
1	FRENCH GP	Clermont-Ferrand	05/07/70	Gold Leaf Team Lotus	Lotus 72-Cosworth DFV	
1	BRITISH GP	Brands Hatch	19/07/70	Gold Leaf Team Lotus	Lotus 72-Cosworth DFV	*Pole*
ret	Trophées de France	Paul Ricard	26/07/70	Jochen Rindt Team Lotus	Lotus 69-Cosworth FVA	*fuel leak*
1	GERMAN GP	Hockenheim	02/08/70	Gold Leaf Team Lotus	Lotus 72-Cosworth DFV	
ret	AUSTRIAN GP	Österreichring	16/08/70	Gold Leaf Team Lotus	Lotus 72-Cosworth DFV	*engine/Pole*
3	Gold Cup–Heat 1	Oulton Park	22/08/70	Gold Leaf Team Lotus	Lotus 72-Cosworth DFV	
1	Gold Cup–Heat 2	Oulton Park	22/08/70	Gold Leaf Team Lotus	Lotus 72-Cosworth DFV	
2	Gold Cup–Aggregate	Oulton Park	22/08/70	Gold Leaf Team Lotus	Lotus 72-Cosworth DFV	
ret	Preis von Salzburg–Heat 1	Salzburgring	30/08/70	Jochen Rindt Team Lotus	Lotus 69-Cosworth FVA	*engine/Pole*
1	Preis von Salzburg–Heat 2	Salzburgring	30/08/70	Jochen Rindt Team Lotus	Lotus 69-Cosworth FVA	*Fastest lap*
13	Preis von Salzburg–Aggregate	Salzburgring	30/08/70	Jochen Rindt Team Lotus	Lotus 69-Cosworth FVA	
dns	ITALIAN GP	Monza	06/09/70	Gold Leaf Team Lotus	Lotus 72-Cosworth DFV	*fatal practice accident*

Formula 1 World Championship positions/points

1965	13th	4
1966	3rd	24
1967	11th=	6
1968	12th	8
1969	4th	22
1970	1st	45
		109

Formula 1 World Championship placings 1st – 6th + Pole + Fastest laps

1st	2nd	3rd	4th	5th	6th	Pole	Fastest lap
6	3	4	6	1	1	10	3

Jochen Rindt's racing record prior to 1964

1961

Started by racing a Simca road car and then purchased a modified Simca, with which he finished third in a national race at Innsbruck.

1962

Raced an Alfa Romeo Giulietta Ti with a lot of success.

1963

Raced Kurt Bardi-Barry's old Cooper-Ford in Formula Junior as Bardi-Barry's team-mate. He gained pole for his first event and won his second at Cesenatico. After that his ability to finish races took a dive, perhaps not unconnected to the fact that Bardi-Barry's mechanics were also his. Unfortunately, from available sources it is not possible at this time to chronicle Rindt's 1963 season in full, so we will have to wait for Paul Sheldon's Formula Junior fact book to discover all the ins and outs of that year.